RUTH AND NAOMI'S

House
of
Bread

by Marion Reid

CRIMOND
HOUSE

CRIMOND HOUSE PUBLICATIONS

"This engaging book captures the original storyline and presents it in an appealing novel way. Although focusing on the entwining consequences of faith, love, adversity and commitment in the lives of Ruth and Naomi, the narrative is resplendent also with rich and relevant Biblical references signposting each one of us to a personal encounter with Jesus Christ, 'The Bread of Life'."
Wilma Barclay, Cookstown

"This isn't a book to be read once and set aside. On the contrary, you must delve into its pages again and again to find rest, comfort and encouragement as you experience dark days of testing and adversity. From Marion's powerful reflections on the lives of Naomi and Ruth you will appreciate more fully the desperate plight of these two Old Testament women and then you can journey with them witnessing their heartache and despair, their courage and faith and eventually their wonderful reward. As you study the carefully chosen Bible passages, let these readings speak into your mind and soul and you will be truly blessed, just as I have been."
Mavis Knox, Broughshane.

"A fresh honest and informative approach to the book of Ruth that will ignite your faith and strengthen your walk."
Wilma Kirk, Templepatrick

"It was a joy to read the wonderful story of the journey of Ruth and Naomi in the Bible and how God was with them giving them the strength to cope with the hardships which they faced.
Marion has portrayed the story in a way that the reader can identify with their experiences and the inclusion of other biblical references makes this book one of great encouragement – a real blessing."
Charlie Smyth, Antrim

Marion can be contacted by:
Email: maranatha30@talktalk.net
Text or phone: 07743924825

Thanks to:

Olive Gardiner who suggested I write a book. Within a few weeks of that conversation I was sitting at my keyboard embarking upon a lifelong ambition. Olive's encouragement came at a time in my life when I was becoming aware of the dawning of a new 'season' in my Christian walk. She has been with me since the first tentative word was written and her enthusiasm and encouragement has been of immense value. During the work on this book we have both walked the pathway of grief several times in our own personal lives and like Ruth and Naomi who shared in sorrow we also have experienced the joy and Grace of our wonderful God.

Wilma, Charlie, Mavis and Wilma who read the manuscript and gave your individual reviews. Being the first people to read what I had written outside of Olive and my publisher caused me to be somewhat nervous as to how you would respond. My fears were soon put to rest with your exciting and refreshing remarks.

Ricky McCoubrey of Crimond House Publications. For all your advice, help and guidance in getting this book into print.

Foreword

It is, with great joy, that I recommend this, Marion's first book, to you its' readers.

It sprang from a casual conversation, over a cup of coffee, which Marion and I shared together after a conference where the seminars were based on the book of Ruth.

The teaching brought to life, in a completely fresh way, this Old Testament story.

I was so impressed I felt others should be able to share something of the excitement of God's working in the lives of ordinary men and women I suggested to Marion her writings should be published.

This book is a feast of encouragement and joy.

May you, the reader, enjoy that feast, in Ruth and Naomi's, House of Bread.

Olive Gardiner

Dear Reader,

My heart's desire is that you would read this book with an open heart and an open Bible.

The intention of writing is not to place in your hands a 'theological or academic' exercise related to the Book of Ruth.

What I would like you to see for yourself are 'ordinary' people living in 'ordinary' circumstances whose lives are touched by our 'extraordinary God.'

The circumstances Ruth and Naomi faced and conquered as they shared in their grief, despair and faith, to some degree may mirror your own and my prayer would be that as you journey on in life, like them, you also would seek to keep on trusting God, even when the road seems bumpy or full of pot-holes.

When troubles come and life seems overwhelming,
keep on trusting.
When discouragement, heartache and pain seems to engulf your very soul,
keep on trusting.
When you feel abandoned, rejected and lonely,
keep on trusting.
When the enemy whispers "Did God really say?"
keep on trusting.

Moving Away

Moving Back

Moving Forward

RUTH Chapter 1

1 In the days when the judges ruled, there was a famine in the land, and a man from Bethlehem in Judah, together with his wife and two sons, went to live for a while in the country of Moab.

2 The man's name was Elimelech, his wife's name Naomi, and the names of his two sons were Mahlon and Kilion. They were Ephrathites from Bethlehem, Judah. And they went to Moab and lived there.

3 Now Elimelech, Naomi's husband, died, and she was left with her two sons.

4 They married Moabite women, one named Orpah and the other Ruth. After they had lived there about ten years,

5 both Mahlon and Kilion also died, and Naomi was left without her two sons and her husband.

6 When she heard in Moab that the LORD had come to the aid of his people by providing food for them, Naomi and her daughters-in-law prepared to return home from there.

7 With her two daughters-in-law she left the place where she had been living and set out on the road that would take them back to the land of Judah.

8 Then Naomi said to her two daughters-in-law, "Go back, each of you, to your mother's home. May the LORD show kindness to you, as you have shown to your dead and to me.

9 May the LORD grant that each of you will find rest in

the home of another husband." Then she kissed them and they wept aloud

10 and said to her, "We will go back with you to your people."

11 But Naomi said, "Return home, my daughters. Why would you come with me? Am I going to have any more sons, who could become your husbands?

12 Return home, my daughters; I am too old to have another husband. Even if I thought there was still hope for me--even if I had a husband tonight and then gave birth to sons--

13 would you wait until they grew up? Would you remain unmarried for them? No, my daughters. It is more bitter for me than for you, because the LORD's hand has gone out against me!"

14 At this they wept again. Then Orpah kissed her mother-in-law good-by, but Ruth clung to her.

15 "Look," said Naomi, "your sister-in-law is going back to her people and her gods. Go back with her."

16 But Ruth replied, "Don't urge me to leave you or to turn back from you. Where you go I will go, and where you stay I will stay. Your people will be my people and your God my God.

17 Where you die I will die, and there I will be buried. May the LORD deal with me, be it ever so severely, if anything but death separates you and me."

18 When Naomi realized that Ruth was determined to go with her, she stopped urging her.

19 So the two women went on until they came to Bethlehem. When they arrived in Bethlehem, the whole town was stirred because of them, and the women exclaimed, "Can this be Naomi?"

20 "Don't call me Naomi, "she told them. "Call me Mara, because the Almighty has made my life very bitter.

21 I went away full, but the LORD has brought me back

empty. Why call me Naomi? The LORD has afflicted me; the Almighty has brought misfortune upon me."

22 So Naomi returned from Moab accompanied by Ruth the Moabitess, her daughter-in-law, arriving in Bethlehem as the barley harvest was beginning.

But you, Bethlehem Ephrathah, though you are small among the clans of Judah, out of you will come for me one who will be ruler over Israel, whose origins are from of old, from ancient times.

Micah 5:2

In that day the Branch of the Lord shall be beautiful and glorious, and the fruit of the land shall be excellent and lovely...

Isaiah 4:2

Then one of the elders said to me, "Do not weep! See, the Lion of the tribe of Judah, the Root of David, has triumphed..."

Revelation 5:5

I Jesus, have sent my angel to give you this testimony for the churches.
I am the Root and the Offspring of David, and the bright Morning Star.

Revelation 22:16

In the very first verse of Ruth Ch1 we read about 'a man from Bethlehem.' This is a very important and intriguing phrase as it sets the scene for the purpose of this short book. Many folk reading this story see it as a sad story with a happy ending or a love story about a poor widow marrying the rich land-owner. All of this is indeed true, but it's more than that, much, much, more. This is a story about the providence and sovereignty of God as He brings about another phase of His great plan of salvation for mankind.

Bethlehem means 'House of Bread' and within the pages of these four chapters we discover some of God's 'treasures of darkness.'

First of all, we meet several characters who are 'men of Bethlehem' all forerunnrs of the most important 'man of Bethlehem' who ever lived, the Man Christ Jesus, who said of himself, *"I Am the Bread of Life."*
Secondly, the story of Ruth doesn't just start in Ch.1, it actually begins at ch 4v17. Let me explain.

> *A shoot will come up from the stump of Jesse; from his roots a Branch will bear fruit*
> **Isaiah 11:1**

Here we discover Jesse - who was the grandson of Ruth. A stump is what is left when a tree is cut down and no matter how long it may take, eventually there appears a shoot!

Sometimes when we think God is doing

17

nothing, we need to remember that all the time, He is doing something.

You see, a shoot doesn't appear all of a sudden, there is a process going on within the stump creating a brand new shoot which will one day spring forth in all its glory. In just the same way as when we look out on our gardens in spring and see leaves, flowers and colour: this didn't happen overnight! It was during the darkness of winter, within the soil or in the bark of the tree that all the work of creation was happening. While on the surface all we could see was dead wood or a space where flowers once grew, underneath the soil and inside bulbs and seeds and branches there was a work going on until one glorious morning new life appeared on the tree or in the bud of a rose!

For centuries God had been at work in the lives of many people, moving towards the moment when Elimelech would leave Bethlehem with his family and when once again the wheels would turn on God's timetable until that glorious day when out of the 'root of Jesse' there would spring forth the shoot;

> Jesus, the Saviour of the world.
> Jesus, the Bread of Life.
> Jesus, the man from Bethlehem,
> the
> ***'House of Bread'***

The role of Ruth and Naomi takes them through the winter of grief, that dark time when God seems distant and uninvolved in their lives until one day, spring bursts open and once again God's song of praise is sung. Yes, he's been there *all the time*, working beneath the surface 'treasures of darkness' as yet undiscovered by them both, but with implications for mankind beyond their imaginations.

Come with me for a visit to

RUTH AND NAOMI'S

House
of
Bread

Moving Away

"For I know the plans I have for you," declares the LORD, "Plans to prosper you and not to harm you, plans to give you a hope and a future."

Jeremiah 29:11

Ruth 1:1-2
In the days when the judges ruled, there was a famine in the land, and a man from Bethlehem in Judea, together with his wife and two sons, went to live for a while in the country of Moab.
The man's name was Elimelech, his wife's name Naomi, and the names of his two sons were Mahlon and Kilion. They were Ephrathites from Bethlehem, Judah. And they went to Moab and lived there.

The first two verses of chapter one in Ruth talk about a family. Ordinary folk doing ordinary things but living in extraordinary circumstances. There was a famine in the land of Israel and they made the decision to move away and live elsewhere until the famine ended. In the providence and sovereignty of God, this decision would have such an effect upon history that the woman whose name graces the title of the book would end up in the lineage of Jesus Christ our Lord and Saviour.

God brought famine when there was disobedience amongst His people. During this period in the history of Israel there were continuous invasions from enemies around them which also led to crop failure and livestock depletion. Unfortunately the innocent suffer with the guilty on occasions such as these.

There is nothing to suggest Elimelech didn't pray and

beg God to bring the famine to an end and it is feasible to suggest they stayed as long as was physically possible. Watching his wife get thinner every day and his children crying out for food he made the most obvious of decisions which was to leave his home and go where food was available. Elimelech took his family to the country of Moab in an effort to keep them alive. Sadly in setting out to preserve all of their lives Elimelech and both his sons died in the land of Moab. The Bible doesn't tell us at what stage of the famine the family moved away but it would mean a long and arduous journey. In order to travel to Moab they would have to walk seventy to eighty miles. Already weakened by lack of food and having to carry whatever belongings they could take, the family probably suffered much hardship along the way.

Moving away from their home, property and extended family would indeed have been emotionally as well as physically draining. Going to live in a strange culture and unfamiliar surroundings would also present many challenges.

Most of us in our western society move house through choice or desire. Some, like Elimelech and his family are forced away because of famine, flood or war, lack of employment opportunities, personal threat to their lives or religious persecution. Whatever the reason, leaving one's home, family and friends to go and live in a strange place can be a daunting experience. Given any other choice very few would want to leave.

Heavenly Father you have promised never to leave us or forsake us. Help us in our decision making to trust you for the outcome. As you seek to fulfil your purposes through us may we 'feed' upon your word and stay close to you. Thank-you for your faithfulness even when we 'move away' from you, in your providential love and care you draw us back to yourself to complete the work you have already begun.

O LORD, you have searched me and you know me. You know when I sit and when I rise; you perceive my thoughts from afar. You discern my going out and my lying down; you are familiar with all my ways.

Before a word is on my tongue you know it completely, O LORD. You hem me in - behind and before; you have laid your hand upon me.Such knowledge is too wonderful for me, too lofty for me to attain.

Where can I go from your Spirit? Where can I flee from your presence? If I go up to the heavens, you are there. If I make my bed in the depths you are there. I f I rise on the wings of the dawn, if I settle on the far side of the sea, even there your hand will guide me, your right hand will hold me fast.

If I say, "Surelythe darkness will hide me and the light become night around me," the night will shine like the day, for darkness is as light to you..

For you created my inmost being; you knit me together in my mother's womb. I praise you because I am fearfully and wonderfully made; Your works are wonderful, I know that full well. My frame was not hidden from you when I was made in the secret place. When I was woven together in the depths of the earth, your eyes saw my unformed body. All the days ordained for me were written in your book before one of them came to be. How precious to me are your thoughts, O God! How vast is the sum of them! Were I to count them they would outnumber the grains of sand. When I awake, I am still with you. Search me O God, and know my heart; test me and know my anxious thoughts, see if there is any offensive way in me, and lead me in the way everlasting.
Psalm 139: 1-18, 23-24

"...I have summoned you by name; you are mine"
Isaiah 43:1

L et us remind ourselves this is a story about ordinary people. The fact that each one of these family members is named shows us that God is interested in individuals and this being so is both encouraging and at the same time, frightening.

> *Encouraging because God is interested in me.*
> *In Heaven, I matter!*
> *Frightening because God knows all about me!*

"What matters supremely, therefore, is not, in the last analysis, the fact that I know God, but the larger fact that underlines it – the fact that -He knows me.
I am graven on the palms of His hands; I am never out of His mind. All my knowledge of Him depends on His sustained initiative in knowing me. I know Him because He first knew me and continues to know me. He knows me as a friend....
There is tremendous relief in knowing that His love to me is utterly realistic based at every point on prior knowledge of the worst about me, so that no discovery can now disillusion Him about me."
J. I. Packer (Knowing God)

This is a statement Naomi could have written because she was a woman who knew her God, and was fully aware that He knew her. And as this story develops, we shall see the evidence of this in her prayers and in her witness.

God's desire for us as individuals is that we become more like His Son Jesus. We can only do this when we spend time in His Word and time in His Presence. This is how we come to know Him, and learn how He would have us live for Him in our daily lives.

Heavenly Father may our hearts respond in thankfulness and praise knowing you see us as individuals and that you treat us as such. Your word tells us that one day we shall see our Saviour face to face and what anticipation should be ours as we wait not only for that day but to learn also of our <u>new</u> name.

*"...I will also give him a white stone with a
new name written on it,
known only to him who receives it"*
Rev.2:17b

Your sun will never set again,
and your moon will wane no more;
the LORD will be your everlasting light,
and your days of sorrow will end.
    Isaiah 60:20

Though he brings grief, he will show compassion, so great is his unfailing love.
For he does not willingly bring affliction or grief to the children of men.
    Lamentations 3:32-33

Ruth 1:3-5
Now Elimelech, Naomi's husband died, and she was left with her two sons.
They married Moabite women, one named Orpah and the other Ruth.
After they had lived there about ten years, both Mahlon and Kilion also died, and Naomi was left without her two sons and her husband.

In the opening verses of Ruth Ch.1 we are introduced to six people and of these, five of them experience the death of a family member. We read that the men all die leaving three widows. Amazingly, there is no account given as to how any of these women felt in their loss, we are left to read between the lines. Naomi had no sons to carry on the family name and both her daughters-in-law were childless. The plight of these three widows was great on every level. They had become destitute in their situation with no men in the family to provide, protect, or care for them. When Naomi lost her husband, her world collapsed. Together they had trekked the seventy plus miles from Bethlehem to Moab with their sons. They had every intention of returning home as a family one day (v.1). Once a wife then a widow and next, a single parent! Disappointment followed soon afterward when both her sons married Moabite women. Surely she had hopes and dreams of them marrying 'nice Hebrew girls' when they got back to Bethlehem. Again further disappointment, when no grand-children arrived into the family and it seemed both her daughters-in-law were barren. Then the ultimate blow, one son died, next the other. What grief this woman had experienced! Her heart broken so many times in just a few short years.

Grief is something we are faced with every day. It is the one statistic that is actually one hundred percent correct, one in one die. Yet in the knowledge of this, grief is traumatic when it happens because along with the grief come many other problems which compound the circumstances. How often have you heard folk say, "I know how you feel…" but they don't know, they can't possibly know! No –one knows how your heart or mine, feels at such times. No-one that is, except the Lord.

"Do not be afraid; you will not suffer shame. Do not fear disgrace; you will not be humiliated. You will forget the shame of your youth and remember no more the reproach of your widowhood. For your Maker is your husband - the LORD ALMIGHTY is His name – the Holy One of Israel is your Redeemer; He is called the God of all the earth…" Isaiah 54:4-5

Heavenly Father, because you are my MAKER, you know exactly how I feel at all times.
Because you are LORD ALMIGHTY you will provide, protect and care for me at all times.
Because you are the Holy One, you want to make me more like Jesus day by day.
Because you are Redeemer, I can stand in your presence covered in the Righteousness of Christ.
Because you are God of all the earth, you are in control of all circumstances concerning me.
Give me the grace I need to bury these truths in my heart to-day.
In Jesus name. Amen.

Jesus Wept.

I will lift up my eyes to the hills – where does my help come from?
My help comes from the LORD, the Maker of heaven and earth.
Psalm 121:1-2

In the gospel of Matthew we read the words of Jesus as He speaks to His disciples in what is known as The Sermon on the Mount.

"Blessed and enviably happy [with a happiness produced by the experience of God's favour and especially conditioned by the revelation of His matchless grace] are those who mourn, for they shall be comforted!"
Matt. 5:4 Amplified

What a verse! Words which at first glance seem to suggest we ought to be happy in our distressing and sorrowful circumstances. On taking a second look however, the end of the verse gives the reason –*"for they shall be comforted."*

The same verse in The Message by Eugene Peterson puts it like this:

"You're blessed when you feel you've lost what is most dear to you. Only then can you be embraced by the One most dear to you."

What lovely words we have in both these verses - blessed, comforted, embraced. These are God's promises to those who mourn. Words Naomi, Orpah and Ruth had yet to experience on a personal level.

When Jesus said, "...shall be," He meant what He said. This is not an empty promise, it is future tense, implying obligation. This comfort will come from Heaven itself! The Apostle Paul talks about this heavenly comfort,

"...He is the God of all comfort" (v.3)
"...who comforts us in all our troubles" (v.4)
2 Cor:1:1-11

Isaiah 61:2-3 says, the LORD will "...comfort all who mourn, and provide for those who grieve in Zion – to bestow on them a crown of beauty instead of ashes, the oil of gladness instead of mourning, and a garment of praise instead of a spirit of despair. They will be called oaks of righteousness, a planting of the LORD for the display of his splendour."

As we progress through the book of Ruth we will see these promises of God being realised in the lives of Naomi and Ruth as they experience for themselves the Grace of God blessing them in ways they never thought possible, comforting them in their trial and embracing them in His love. In our pain may we 'taste and see that the LORD is good' (Ps.34:8) and as Paul reminds us 'the Lord comforts us so that we can comfort others with the comfort which we ourselves have received.'(2Cor1:4b)

Heavenly Father, whether it's grief, disappointment, discouragement, loneliness, despair, or some other trial we are going through, help us to turn to the One who can sympathise with us in our weaknesses and impart that promised comfort. Surely this is how we are Blessed and enviably happy! In Jesus name. Amen.

Do not hurry
as you walk with grief
it does not help the journey.

Walk slowly
pausing often:
Do not hurry
as you walk with grief.

Do not be disturbed
By memories that come unbidden
swiftly forgive:
And let Christ speak for you
unspoken words.
Unfinished conversation
will be resolved in Him.
Do not be disturbed.

Be gentle with the One
who walks with grief.
If it is you
Be gentle with yourself.
Swiftly forgive
Walk slowly
Pausing often.
Take time, be gentle
As you walk with grief.

Moving Back

The LORD
is my light and my salvation
whom shall I fear?

The LORD
is the stronghold of my life
of whom shall I be afraid?

One thing I ask of
the LORD,
this is what I seek:

that I may dwell in the house of
the LORD
all the days of my life,

to gaze upon the beauty of
the LORD
and to seek him in his temple.

For in the day of trouble
he will keep me safe in his dwelling
he will hide me in the
shelter of his tabernacle
and set me high upon a rock.
Ps. 27:1,4,5

When she heard in Moab that the LORD had come to the aid of his people by providing food for them, Naomi and her daughters-in-law prepared to return home from there.
RUTH CH 1 VS 6

Naomi left Bethlehem the 'House of Bread' to look for bread, some years ago and now she had heard news which would draw her back home, 'The LORD had come to the aid of his people.' How comforting these words are – 'The LORD'

In the circumstances which surround us in this life some of which bring heartache and trouble, isn't it wonderful to know that 'The LORD' comes to the aid of His people. When we put our faith and trust in the Lord Jesus Christ to have our sins forgiven the Bible says to us:

"How great is the love the Father has lavished on us, that we should be called children of God!" And that is what we are!
1 John 3:1 N.I.V

There are two exclamation marks in this statement. It is as if John is experiencing this truth for the very first time and is caught up in the wonder of it all and what a wonder it is that the LORD should love us so. Being a child of God should give us the most amazing sense of belonging, with the knowledge of what it is to be truly loved, accepted and forgiven. The fact that God

41

has chosen to place us as members in his family, accept us as his children and treat us as such, should cause us to lift up our voices in praise and thanksgiving.

As one of the covenant children of God Naomi chose to go home and, with her daughters-in-law began to make preparations. How intriguing to read, 'she left the place'(v.7.) Moab had only ever been a temporary dwelling place for Naomi - it wasn't 'home.'

They say home is where the heart is and for Naomi home was where God was, and the true God of Heaven was the God of Israel. Her real home was with her God and God's covenant people.

Moving back would have been a very emotional decision for all of them. First of all they had to decide what to take with them as they would walk over seventy miles in unforgiving terrain. Secondly, particularly for Naomi, they would be leaving their whole family behind in their graves in Moab.

For most folk, walking away from the grave of a loved one is the hardest part in the grief process. For Naomi, Ruth and Orpah, who perhaps visited their graves and left flowers, paused a while and pondered how life used to be, they now had to walk away, leaving graves which they would never attend again. Those they had loved so dearly they had to let go. In the letting go, they were closing a chapter on each of their lives and beginning a walk into an unknown future without their men. Letting go was not easy but it was necessary, mainly because, in the providence of God, He was calling Naomi back.

Father God help us to realize that this earth is not our home when our lives have been redeemed by the precious blood of Jesus. You are preparing a place for your children. A glorious new home where we will see you face to face and be forever in your Presence.

"... I go to prepare a place for you, and if I go and prepare a place for you, I will come back and take you to be with me that you also may be where I am"
John 14:2

Religion that God our Father accepts as pure and faultless is this: to look after orphans and widows in their distress.
James 1:27

***With her two daughters-in-law she left the place where she had been living and set out on the road that would take them back to the land of Judah.*
Ruth 1:7**

The three women begin their journey back to Bethlehem Judah. Their widowhood evident to all as it was etched on their faces and displayed by their clothing. In the culture of the book of Ruth a woman's significance was determined by her having a husband and bearing children, especially sons. Naomi later told the women of Bethlehem that she 'went away full' but came back 'empty' (v21). Bereft of both her husband and sons Naomi's life was greatly diminished, her status in the community was reduced to the lowest rung on the ladder and as she walked that road, her thoughts were centred on what lay ahead especially concerning her daughters-in-law, as they too had no husbands and no children.

Naomi also knew that the widow could only marry a male relative of her dead husband, and as these girls were foreigners, that was going to prove a difficulty. They would be ostracised even more. Her fears for the future were real and not imagined and she was concerned for the safety of these young women who could fall into the hands of all sorts of predators from any angle of society.

The Hebrew word for widow (almanah) gave definition to her place in society. It comes from the root word alem, which means "unable to speak." The widow was incapable of seeking justice on any level. Without a father, husband or son, or indeed any other male relative to play advocate, she herself had no voice, no legal rights and no defence against any injustices which would come her way. She was also categorised among the most vulnerable members of society - widows, orphans and foreigners.

Naomi was willing to walk the long journey home all alone rather than subject her daughters-in-law to a life of poverty and most likely, racial and social abuse. Her desire was to see them find love and happiness again regardless of any dangers and fears she may have to face personally by journeying on alone. Overwhelmed by all of this Naomi turns to her daughters-in-law and exclaims, *"Go back..." (v.8).*

Widows in some cultures even in our world to-day are treated as outcasts, forced to live and beg on the streets, to shave their heads and wear clothing which defines their status. There are always those who will prey on the vulnerable and the weak. Women and young girls trafficked for all sorts of reasons, girl babies left on rubbish heaps simply because they are girls, and on it goes.

Heavenly Father help us to be willing always, to look out for the good of others and not be selfish in seeking only what satisfies ourselves. Naomi could so easily have played the 'poor me' but she thought of her daughters-in-law and their welfare and that is commendable under the circumstances.

May we pray for and consider the plight of those who are weak, vulnerable and destitute, even in our own family, community, or Church.

Large crowds were travelling with Jesus, and turning to them he said:

"If anyone comes to me and does not hate his father and mother, his wife and children, his brothers and sisters -yes, even his own life - he cannot be my disciple.

And anyone who does not carry his cross and follow me cannot be my disciple.

In the same way, any of you who does not give up everything he has cannot be my disciple."

Luke Ch. 14:26,27,33.

*At this they wept again. Then Orpah kissed
her mother-in-law goodbye...*
Ruth Ch. 1 v 14

At the end of v.9 we read of tears being shed. This is the first time tears are actually mentioned even after all the grief these three women have been through. No doubt there had been many tears in the past, but the tears shed by Orpah and Ruth were because they could not imagine complete severance of any connection to Naomi and the suggestion from Naomi, that they return to their mother's homes is almost too hard to bear. They wept aloud. What a sight that must have been to the onlooker. Two young women, broken-hearted, as they contemplate parting from their mother-in-law.

Mother's-in-law for the most part as we know it, are the brunt of jokes and funny stories. Yet here, the relationship takes on a whole new meaning.

Because of their marriages to Naomi's sons, Orpah and Ruth are duty- bound to their mother-in-law. In the Hebrew culture a woman was bound to her husband's family even after his death and a woman could return to her family only if her purchase price was paid to her husband's heirs. Naomi was willing to give these women opportunity to relinquish this bond when she looked at the circumstances facing them in Bethlehem should they continue the journey. Orpah and Ruth resisted this suggestion at first by proclaiming, "We will go back with you to your people." (v10) Regardless of their obvious devotion Naomi spelt out very practically what their future looked like, (vs. 11-13.)

Orpah, whose name means; youthful, freshness, had spent some years in the home of the covenant people of God. She had witnessed their observance of God's laws and heard their prayers. She knew their God was not like the false gods of Moab (especially the god Chemosh to whom child sacrifice was made) yet, here on the road to Judah she looks at life from her own perspective and figures she doesn't want to spend any more time in misery and abject poverty. She doesn't want to lose her looks too early and be dressed forever in widow's garb. No, the life Orpah desires, even amongst the gods of Moab, looks much more inviting. Orpah makes her decision. She weighs up the situation, and it looks as if going on is not an option for her. She wants a future, a husband, a home, a family. So she accepts the offer of freedom, weeps again, kisses her mother-in-law goodbye and turns back to Moab.

Heavenly Father, help us to make good choices in life even though we do not see the way ahead too clearly. Often our perspective is clouded by our own wants and desires. All Orpah could see ahead were negatives. Her decision to 'go back' separated her not only from Naomi and Ruth but also from the blessing of God and the promise of a Heavenly home.

Had our LORD and Saviour 'gone back' none of us would ever be born again into the family of God. Rather "They were on their way up to Jerusalem, with Jesus leading the way..." (Mk.10:32)
Praise God Jesus walked the long road home. He wouldn't and couldn't turn back because "while we were still sinners, Christ died for us." (Rom. 5 v 8b)

Where would we be without Him?

By this all men will know that
you are my disciples,
if you love one another.
John 13:35

But Ruth clung to her.
Ruth 1:14

Somewhere along that road Naomi, Orpah and Ruth, came to a crossroads. Not a physical one but a spiritual one. Orpah has already made her choice and is now walking away in the opposite direction from Bethlehem. Ruth on the other hand, is standing there clinging to her mother-in-law Naomi. As they watch the lone figure of Orpah moving further and further away, Naomi exclaims, "Look, your sister-in-law is going back to her people and her gods. Go back with her." This is now the fourth time Naomi has mentioned 'going back.'

Like Orpah, Ruth had observed the way of life of this Hebrew family into which she married. During their 'little while' in Moab Ruth had seen and heard enough to make her realise that the religion of the Moabites did not include a god which was real and personal, who heard and answered prayer and who provided food for His people. Ruth had also been thinking as she walked the road that day and when faced with the request of Naomi to go back, she was ready to respond. And what a response! (vs.16,17)

Ruth tells Naomi to stop urging her to leave and go back. She pledges to stay with her mother-in-law wherever she goes, wherever she stays. Ruth goes on to commit herself to the Hebrew way of life by trusting in the God of Naomi. At this point, Ruth has confessed faith in the living and true God and is putting her future in His hands. She then adds another dimension to her commitment to Naomi, "Where you die I will die, and there I will be buried". In other words, Ruth determined that Naomi would not be alone in this life and even though the 'family plot' was now in Moab, there would be a new one in Bethlehem and Naomi could be assured of this. Ruth's final words of devotion came when she prayed her very first prayer, "May the Lord deal with me, be it ever so severely, if anything but death separates you and me."

When Naomi realised that Ruth was determined to go with her she stopped urging her' (v.18.) What love this young woman showed for her mother-in-law and what an example Naomi must have been for Ruth to make such a statement! On the road to Bethlehem Ruth put her faith and trust in God. She gave up her home, family and culture, and was prepared to face the unknown as she turned once again in the direction of Bethlehem, 'The House of Bread,' and began again on the long road home.

Heavenly Father, being a witness for you is not reserved for the good times in our lives, but also in times of difficulty and adversity. May we, like Naomi, display our faith at all times so that others, regardless of race or culture may see You at work in and through our lives that they too, may come like Ruth and put their faith and trust in You. Help us to say like Paul,

"....for I have learned to be content whatever the circumstances.... I have learned the secret of being content in any and every situation.... I can do everything through him who gives me strength."
Phil.4:11-14

There is a time for everything, and a
season for every activity under heaven:
A time to be born and a time to die,
a time to plant and a time to uproot,
a time to kill and a time to heal,
a time to tear down and a time to build,
a time to weep and a time to laugh,
a time to mourn and a time to dance,
a time to scatter stones
and a time to gather them,
a time to embrace and a time to refrain,
a time to search and a time to give up,
a time to keep and a time to throw away,
a time to tear and a time to mend,
a time to be silent and a time to speak,
a time to love and a time to hate,
a time for war and a time for peace.
He has made everything beautiful in its time.
Ecclesiastes Ch.3:1-8; 11

So the two women went on until they
came to Bethlehem...
Ruth 1:19

Naomi and Ruth had a long way to go as they set out once again on the road home to Bethlehem. With the family of six now reduced to two, they walked perhaps in silence for a while, then some conversation and most definitely, more tears. Tears happen in all kinds of situations not just the sad times. We shed tears at the sight of a new-born baby, we cry at weddings or even when our children and grand-children achieve in personal and positive areas of their lives and in many other 'happy' circumstances. Yet tears are something that so very often we are reluctant to shed. A stiff upper lip attitude keeps tears locked away; maybe the thought of embarrassment or awkwardness in certain situations cause us to keep control of our emotions. Whatever reason we may have, God, when creating man-kind created tearducts! it is with this in mind that I am reminded of the words of David:

"...the Lord has heard my weeping" Ps.6:8

"You number and record my wanderings; put my tears into Your bottle – are they not in your book" Ps.56:8 Amplified

How comforting these verses are:
God sees our tears,
He hears our weeping.
He has a 'vessel' into which He puts those tears
and not only that,
He records them in His book.

Our tears do not go unnoticed in Heaven.

While Naomi and Ruth walk and talk as they go along the road, tear stained eyes glance at each other from time to time as they discuss when to rest, where to eat, maybe even what to eat. It probably wasn't very clear to them, at this point in time that they were walking away from their season of winter into the light of spring. The dark days of despondency were now behind them and with each mile they trod they were being drawn more and more towards the Grace, Love and Gentle Heart of the One who whispers,

"Your Maker is your Husband..." Isaiah 54:5a

In order to wipe away tears from a child's eye the parent stoops down, cups the little one's face in their hand and lifts the tear stained face upwards. What a picture of what God will do one day for His children!

And God shall wipe away all tears from their eyes; and there shall be no more death, neither sorrow, nor crying, neither shall there be any more pain: for the former things are passed away. Rev.20:4

Father God, when we are stooped in sadness, grief, discouragement or whatever, and the 'hard stuff' in life is difficult to bear, Your Word is what makes the difference. It lifts our hearts, encourages our souls and shows us Someone cares. Help us to take Your words of hope, comfort and promise, and apply them in our situations so that we can know we are not walking this road alone.

Now that same day two of them were going to a village called Emmaus, about seven miles from Jerusalem. They were talking with each other about everything that had happened. As they talked and discussed these things with each other, Jesus himself came up and walked along with them; but they were kept from recognising him.

He asked them, "What are you discussing together as you walk along?" They stood still, their faces downcast. One of them, named Cleopas, asked him, "Are you only a visitor to Jerusalem and do not know the things that have happened there in these days?" "What things?" he asked. "About Jesus of Nazareth," they replied. "He was a prophet, powerful in word and deed before God and all the people. The chief priests and our rulers handed him over to be sentenced to death, and they crucified him; but we had hoped that he was the one who was going to redeem Israel. And what is more, it is the third day since all this took place. In addition, some of our women amazed us. They went to the tomb early this morning but didn't find his body. They came and told us that they had seen a vision of angels, who said he was alive. Then some of our companions went to the tomb and found it just as the women had said, but him they did not see."

He said to them, "How foolish you are, and how slow of heart to believe all that the prophets have spoken. Did not the Christ have to suffer these things and enter his glory?" And beginning with Moses and all the Prophets, he explained to them what was said in all the Scriptures concerning himself.

As they approached the village to which they were going, Jesus acted as if he were going further. But they urged him strongly, "Stay with us, for it is nearly evening; the day is almost over." So he went in to stay with them. When he was at the table with them, he took bread, gave thanks, broke it and began to give it to them. Then their eyes were opened and they recognised him, and he disappeared from their sight. They asked each other, "Were not our hearts burning within us while he talked with us on the road and opened the Scriptures to us?

They got up and returned at once to Jerusalem. There they found the Eleven and those with them, assembled together and saying, "It is true! The Lord has risen and has appeared to Simeon." Then the two told what had happened on the way, and how Jesus was recognised by them when he broke the bread.

Luke Ch.24: 13-35

***So the two women went on until they came
to Bethlehem...***
Ruth 1:19

The journey of Naomi and Ruth reminds me very much of the two disciples on the road to Emmaus. As they walked and talked about the events which had happened in Jerusalem regarding the death of Jesus Christ I venture to suggest they walked slowly, dragging their heels, looking at the ground and feeling very empty. Then a stranger drew up alongside them and entered into their conversation. With downcast faces, they stopped and looked at him in disbelief. They couldn't understand why he didn't know anything about what had taken place over the previous couple of days. In fact, what they didn't know was, that the one to whom they were speaking was Jesus Himself, now risen from the dead as He had told them beforehand but He kept them from recognizing Him. Do you ever wonder why this was? Well it may be that their faith in the Word of God was being tested. As the stranger asked them to tell him of the things which happened, their explanation was full of negative words;

"He was"(v.19)

　"But we had hoped"

　　"that he was the one who was, and what is more, it is

　　the third day since all this took place"(v.21)

　　　"...they didn't find his body"(v.23)

The two disciples talked in past tense and were very negative. Their grief had clouded their thinking. They had not remembered anything Jesus had taught them. They even skimmed over the fact that angels appeared to the women. Isn't it is amazing when, in our times of distress, we can't think straight or see things in their proper perspective. The stranger did not let them off the hook too easily when in he rebukes them for their unbelief and then goes on to preach the truth of the Scriptures to them: and all of it concerning Jesus (Himself) and His sufferings, His death and resurrection!(v.25) Later in the account we read that they finally realized it was Jesus who walked and talked with them on the road and on the discovery of this they said to each other, "Were not our hearts *burning* within us while he talked with us on the road and *opened_the Scriptures* to us? I think that as Ruth and Naomi walked towards Bethlehem and away from Moab, that the Lord Himself came and walked alongside. No, they couldn't see Him but He was there nonetheless, in their hearts, through the promises of His Word and for Ruth, a spark of HOPE was being kindled in her heart.

Father God, Your Presence is what we need in our daily lives and You have given it to us by Your Holy Spirit living within us, yet how faithless we can be at times. May we spend time in Your Word building up our faith so that in the difficulties and trials, that Word will be the anchor for our souls, lifting us up to a higher place, soaring with You, standing on the promises and believing you are near.

At the end of the journey tired as they were the disciples got up and returned at once to Jerusalem,

What made the difference?   -   the Word of GOD
Who made the difference?   -   the Presence of Jesus

Though you have not seen him, you love him; and even though you do not see him now, you believe in him and are filled with an inexpressible and glorious joy, for you are receiving the goal of your faith, the salvation of your souls.

I Peter 1; 8-9

Then Jesus told him, "Because you have seen me, you have believed; blessed are those who have not seen and yet have believed."

John 20:29

1 Corinthians 3:9
No eye has seen, no ear has heard, no mind conceived what God has prepared for those who love him.

Returning to Bethlehem meant they had to cross the river Jordan. This would be a defining moment in Ruth's life. Crossing over the river is the final step for her into a new world. Her ties with Moab would most definitely be severed. She has, by the providence of God been brought into a new community, she will be called by a new name, live in a new family and set up a new home. All this awaits the young Moabitess who, through her marriage and subsequent grief, has found a new God – Yahweh – in whom she has entrusted her future.

Some years before this, Naomi's ancestors had crossed the same river under the leadership of Joshua. Having been commissioned in the plains of Moab by Moses, he lead the Hebrews to the promised land, a land flowing with milk and honey. A land designated by God as their inheritance. Egypt was put away forever now, and by crossing over Jordan, they were entering into a new land, full of promise and opportunity. Into a place of blessing and abundance, should they walk in the ways of God.

Perhaps as they crossed the river, Naomi related some of the family history in this respect and explained to Ruth why the Hebrews were God's chosen people. Ruth, on the other hand, would be aware that by her confession of faith in this same God, she too, would enter into the blessings which that faith afforded and once again hope was kindled in her heart, the hope of something better. This hope was that both she and her mother-in-law would be 'remembered' by God, and that He, in some way or other would bring about a change in their circumstances. Her new found faith, immature as it was, could see that obedience brings blessing, and in Ruth's heart, she committed her life to God.

How precious it is to remember when we first came to faith ourselves, we believed anything was possible! And it is! It's just that somewhere along life's journey, as we climb over the bumps in the road, we seem to lose some of that exuberant faith which was so evident when first we came to know the Lord.

Coming into Bethlehem on that spring day, Ruth must have experienced a mix of anticipation along with the fear of the unknown. Unaware of how she would be received in her new community, or how she and Naomi would live from day to day she nevertheless knew this, the Lord had provided food for His people in Bethlehem, the' House of Bread,' and that was the reason they were 'home.'

Heavenly Father, there are many ways in which you draw people to yourself and regardless of anything else, you require that we give our all to you. Ruth left her past behind in Moab and willingly came. Coming with empty hands, an empty heart and little faith, she had all the ingredients necessary in order for You to do a great work in her life. Help us to-day, to lay aside self and come like Ruth believing You for the blessing in whatever we face to-day.

Therefore if anyone is in Christ, he is a new creation; the old has gone, the new has come. 2 Cor: 5:17

The LORD your God is with you, He is mighty to save.
He will take great delight in you,
He will quiet you with His love,
He will rejoice over you with singing.
    Zephaniah 3;17

But I have stilled and quietened my soul;
like a weaned child with its mother,
like a weaned child is my soul within me.
    Psalm 131:2

Ruth 1:22
So Naomi returned from Moab, accompanied by Ruth the Moabitess, her daughter-in-law, arriving in Bethlehem as the barley harvest was beginning.

After a tired dusty hungry and heart-wrenching walk, the two women arrive at their destination, the little town of Bethlehem. For Naomi, there was a sense of rest on one hand, and overwhelming loss on the other. Rest because she was home. Isn't home the place we find relaxation, comfort, and an air of security. The people we love are there and after a journey or a time away how we enjoy sharing all the experiences we have encountered. Overwhelming loss because there was no-one there! The house would be empty and cold, probably in an unkempt state also, having been unoccupied for the last ten years. No laughter ringing within its walls, no washing to pick up off the floor, no hugs, kisses, or any kind of intimate contact. Her beloved husband gone, her two lovely sons - gone.

Walking beside her mother-in-law, Ruth takes in her new surroundings.There was a great deal of activity going on around them. Singing filled the air, children played and danced in the streets. Everyone was busy preparing for the gathering in of the harvest. Yes, God had provided for His people again. It was indeed a time of rejoicing. A time to praise God with thanksgiving for the harvest just as God had commanded them to do when He brought their ancestors out of slavery all those years ago and gave them this land. (Lev.23:9-14)

Ruth stands with her eyes closed, face to the sun, thanking God quietly in her own heart as the sound of singing fills her ears. These were God songs. Songs she had never heard before. Songs of deliverance, redemption, faithfulness, love, compassion and peace fall like a blanket around her gathering her up in its folds and holding her in its embrace. Ruth had not sung in a long time and what a welcome it was to her as she entered into a new phase in her life.

Ruth had come home spiritually speaking, home in her heart to God. She found His peace, comfort and strength, and she knew instinctively that everything was going to be alright. This God is in the business of renewal, not only in nature, but in the hearts of ordinary men and women. She was learning to sing again! The hope which had begun to burn in her heart along the road was now becoming a reality.

Psalm 91 is referred to as the 'Song of Ruth' and as she stands at the entrance to Bethlehem this young Moabitess was claiming in effect the words of v.4:

> **"He will cover you with His feathers. And under His wings you will find refuge;"**

LORD, how difficult it is for us to find our song when troubles invade and our world crashes in.
I thank You to-day that even when I cannot sing, You are singing over me!
Just like a parent soothing a troubled child, my strength returns and I am refreshed once again.
What a privilege it is to call you
"Abba Father"

But you, O Sovereign LORD, deal well with me for your name's sake; out of the goodness of your love, deliver me. For I am poor and needy, and my heart is wounded within me. I fade away like an evening shadow; I am shaken off like a locust. My knees give way from fasting; my body is thin and gaunt.

I am an object of scorn to my accusers; when they see me, they shake their heads. With my mouth I will greatly extol the LORD; in the great throng I will praise him. For he stands at the right hand of the needy one, to save his life from those who condemn him.

Psalm 109:21-25 ;30, 31

Ruth 1:19-21
....When they arrived in Bethlehem, the whole town was stirred because of them, and the women exclaimed, "Can this be Naomi?"

Naomi had been through a time in her life which, most definitely, caused her to question her faith. Yet as we have already seen she didn't give up on God. Yes, she had struggled through the tough questions, "Where is God? What is He doing? Does He not see what's going on here! If I am His child, why is this happening to me?" Questions she probably would never get an answer to but she asked them just the same. When her husband died she asked. When one of her sons died she asked. When the other son died she asked. No answer from Heaven for Naomi and yet, it was this same shattered faith which seemingly spoke volumes to Ruth because she saw in Naomi someone who didn't get answers but who still trusted the true God of Heaven. As she stands before her friends and neighbours of a decade ago and they ask, "Can this be Naomi?" her response is very quick and comes from an empty space somewhere deep within. I can imagine her waving her hands backwards and forwards, motioning to her hearers as she says to them, "Don't call me Naomi, call me Mara....."

Her name Naomi means sweet, pleasant, but right now she didn't see anything pleasant about herself. She decides to change her name to Mara, meaning bitter, unpleasant. She sees herself in a different way now than when she first left Bethlehem. Back then she was 'full' now she is 'empty.' The bitterness comes not from an attitude of bitterness, but from bitter experiences. There is a difference. Proverbs 14:10 which says, 'each heart knows its own bitterness, and no-one else can share its joy' has the same Hebrew word for bitterness as the word used here by Naomi.

Three lives taken from one home is something most of us cannot even imagine happening. To be left as Naomi was, totally bereft of support, protection and status, she feels that pleasantness doesn't even begin to describe her.

How could anyone be pleasant in these circumstances? Naomi had indeed been been drinking from bitter waters. Her heart has been deeply wounded and the name Mara explains without words how she is feeling right now.

Father God, there are times we too feel like Mara's because of bitter circumstances in our own lives.

Help us to remember what You call us:
a chosen people
a royal priesthood
a holy nation
a people belonging to God…

May we stand on <u>this</u> platform when the bitter experiences come our way.
1Peter2:9a

Come, let us bow down in worship, let us kneel before the LORD our Maker; for he is our God and we are the people of his pasture, the flock under his care.

Psalm 95:6-7

Ruth 1:19-21
....When they arrived in Bethlehem, the whole town was stirred because of them...

The reason for Naomi's 'Mara' moment was the fact that the whole town seemed to know of her arrival and that she was back on her own except for the Moabitess. Isn't it the case, when we are in times of sorrow and grief and at our most vulnerable, when folk arrive to visit or draw alongside to comfort we suddenly break down and begin to feel the weight of it all. With a large audience before her I think Naomi gave a pretty good account of her situation. There are some who would say that she blamed God, was a bitter woman, was angry at God yet, reading again what she said tells me she was a woman who knew her God.

The God of her forefathers.

The God she had been taught about from her childhood.

The God who was also the God of those listening to her – YAHWEH – the covenant God of Israel. They knew exactly what she meant when she said;

> *"....the Almighty has made my life very bitter/the LORD has brought me back empty/ the LORD has afflicted me/the Almighty has brought misfortune upon me."*

There may have times when she privately asked the "Why" questions, but here, before God's people her faith announces 'Who' is in control. She knows God is sovereign in all and every circumstance of life and she acknowledges Him in His dealings with her. Yes, she was hurting, yes, she was stripped bare of all her 'props' so to speak, yes, she stood in a lonely place, a desert place, but God had allowed all of this to happen, and she knew it. His divine purposes were beyond the control of Naomi and she, by referring to Him as both LORD and Almighty, would have also known Him as the One who was always present with His people, always near, and always working out His purposes for their ultimate good and His Glory. The sufferings of this life, as far as Naomi was concerned, were part of the journey and she was not so much shaking her fist in the air at God but rather, in her state of despondency and vulnerability, just lay down underneath the weight of it all.

I see a bruised, battered and broken woman standing on the street in Bethlehem that day, and yet, she was testifying of God's hand in her life and was prepared to acknowledge that along with the good things in life, there also comes the sorrow.

Two widowed, childless women standing together; one whose heart is beginning to sing again, the other, struggling in her faith, yet holding on to the God of Abraham to whom she now needs to look for her own personal deliverance and be saved from what looks like a very bleak future.

The name YAHWEH speaks of the One who delivered and saved His covenant people out of Egypt and brought them to the land of promise. God Almighty in Hebrew is EL Shadday, the all-sufficient One. This is the God of the 'impossible'

Heavenly Father, in our days of brokenness it can be difficult even to pray let alone tell others about you. Help us to keep our focus on WHO You really are; The all-powerful, all-sufficient God, for whom nothing is impossible.

We wait in hope for the LORD;
he is our help and shield.
In him our hearts rejoice,
for we trust in his holy name.
May your unfailing love rest upon us, O Lord,
even as we put our hope in you.
    Psalm 33:20-22

Ruth 1:22
So Naomi returned from Moab accompanied by Ruth the Moabitess, her daughter-in-law, arriving in Bethlehem as the barley harvest was beginning.

The Book of Ruth is the eighth book in the Bible and according to some scholars the number eight denotes new beginnings. Back on the road hope had been kindled in Ruth's heart, the hope of something better. The courage to give up her home, culture and country was based on what she knew of Namoi's God. This led her to a new found faith in the God of Israel and deep commitment to her mother-in-law. Verse twenty-two sits in stark contrast to the opening verse of this chapter. At that time Naomi, as she said herself "went away full..." now with her grief still raw, any hope for the future lay buried inside a wounded heart.

Little did either she or Ruth know they were standing on the threshold of God's Amazing grace because, even though Naomi said she had come back 'empty' the reality was the exact opposite. God had reached into Moab and brought out from there a young woman who would grace the pages of Holy Writ, whose name would be recorded in the lineage of Jesus our Saviour and whose name is still mentioned to-day, centuries later, as the book of Ruth is read by Jewish communities around the world at the Feast of Pentecost.

Naomi was very 'full' if she only but knew it and the next forty-nine days would change both of these women's lives forever because the Bible tells us that, 'Ruth gleaned in the fields of Boaz until the barley and wheat harvests were finished' (ch2:43 - a period of forty-nine days.)

Again we sense the anticipation of Ruth and the despair of Naomi, yet the story is drawing us in on a personal level as we, also, sense the Presence of the unseen God, silently, graciously and gently standing with them as they are met by the townsfolk of Bethlehem.

As the two women would settle down to life back in Bethlehem unsure of what the future held, one of them had already purposed in her heart to lay hold of the God of Israel and prove Him for herself. Ruth was a woman who had faith to believe that the stories she had heard about YAHWEH, were of a God who was powerful and could do the impossible and her future rested on these truths.

The two widows now take centre stage under God's spotlight as His great plan of salvation continues to unfold.

Father God, may we take up Your word afresh to-day and re-read those same accounts, so that in our trials and tribulations faith will rise with renewed hope in You and in Your Word.
The word of promise which can sustain us in all our ways.
Jesus said we would have tribulation in this world but the comfort He gives us is this,
"But take heart! I have overcome the world." (John 17:33b)
Thank-you Father for these words of victory. Help us to live according to that word regardless of all that's going on in our lives to-day.

Now faith is being sure of what we hope for and certain of what we do not see. Heb. 11:1

Moving Forward

RUTH Chapter 2

1 Now Naomi had a relative on her husband's side, from the clan of Elimelech, a man of standing, whose name was Boaz.

2 And Ruth the Moabitess said to Naomi, "Let me go to the fields and pick up the leftover grain behind anyone in whose eyes I find favor." Naomi said to her, "Go ahead, my daughter."

3 So she went out and began to glean in the fields behind the harvesters. As it turned out, she found herself working in a field belonging to Boaz, who was from the clan of Elimelech.

4 Just then Boaz arrived from Bethlehem and greeted the harvesters, "The LORD be with you!" "The LORD bless you!" they called back.

5 Boaz asked the foreman of his harvesters, "Whose young woman is that?"

6 The foreman replied, "She is the Moabitess who came back from Moab with Naomi.

7 She said, 'Please let me glean and gather among the sheaves behind the harvesters.' She went into the field and has worked steadily from morning till now, except for a short rest in the shelter."

8 So Boaz said to Ruth, "My daughter, listen to me. Don't go and glean in another field and don't go away from here. Stay here with my servant girls.

9 Watch the field where the men are harvesting, and follow along after the girls. I have told the men not to

touch you. And whenever you are thirsty, go and get a drink from the water jars the men have filled."

10 At this, she bowed down with her face to the ground. She exclaimed, "Why have I found such favor in your eyes that you notice me--a foreigner?"

11 Boaz replied, "I've been told all about what you have done for your mother-in-law since the death of your husband--how you left your father and mother and your homeland and came to live with a people you did not know before.

12 May the LORD repay you for what you have done. May you be richly rewarded by the LORD, the God of Israel, under whose wings you have come to take refuge."

13 "May I continue to find favor in your eyes, my lord," she said. "You have given me comfort and have spoken kindly to your servant--though I do not have the standing of one of your servant girls."

14 At mealtime Boaz said to her, "Come over here. Have some bread and dip it in the wine vinegar." When she sat down with the harvesters, he offered her some roasted grain. She ate all she wanted and had some left over.

15 As she got up to glean, Boaz gave orders to his men, "Even if she gathers among the sheaves, don't embarrass her.

16 Rather, pull out some stalks for her from the bundles and leave them for her to pick up, and don't rebuke her."

17 So Ruth gleaned in the field until evening. Then she threshed the barley she had gathered, and it amounted to about an ephah.

18 She carried it back to town, and her mother-in-law saw how much she had gathered. Ruth also brought out and gave her what she had left over after she had eaten enough.

19 Her mother-in-law asked her, "Where did you glean

today? Where did you work? Blessed be the man who took notice of you!" Then Ruth told her mother-in-law about the one at whose place she had been working. "The name of the man I worked with today is Boaz," she said.

20 "The LORD bless him!" Naomi said to her daughter-in-law. "He has not stopped showing his kindness to the living and the dead." She added, "That man is our close relative; he is one of our kinsman-redeemers."

21 Then Ruth the Moabitess said, "He even said to me, 'Stay with my workers until they finish harvesting all my grain.' "

22 Naomi said to Ruth her daughter-in-law, "It will be good for you, my daughter, to go with his girls, because in someone else's field you might be harmed."

23 So Ruth stayed close to the servant girls of Boaz to glean until the barley and wheat harvests were finished. And she lived with her mother-in-law.

Be at rest once more, O my soul,
for the LORD has been good to you.
Ps. 116:7

Shout for joy, O heavens; rejoice O earth;
For the LORD comforts his people
and will have compassion on his afflicted ones.
— Isaiah 49:13

So Naomi returned from Moab accompanied by Ruth the Moabitess, her daughter-in-law, arriving in Baethlehem as the barley harvest was beginning.
Ruth1:22
So Ruth stayed close to the servant girls of Boaz to glean until the barley and wheat harvests were finished.
Ruth 2:23

Once we leave behind the first chapter of Ruth there is a distinct shift in gear. The first chapter held us in the grip of grief, despair and loss and even though those things haven't changed for Ruth and Naomi we discover on their return to Bethlehem that their lives take on a much different pace, they are swept away on a tide of renewed hope and expectation as they stand in awe of the grace of God providing for their needs in a way beyond anything they ever envisioned.

'Moving on' begins as soon as they arrive back in Naomi's home town. Nothing is standing still for them. Every day is filled with joy and excitement and wonder. Suddenly they are seeing possibilities of a brighter future, one which will allow them to even dare to dream and sing and dance again. The days of brokenness and loneliness are swallowed up with a renewed sense of purpose, even Naomi, whose personal grief, pain and bitterness of soul caused her to change her name, now seems to be living on the edge of anticipation rather than just marking time.

Seven weeks is the time Ruth spent in the fields of

Boaz as she worked to support herself and Naomi. This particular period falls between Passover and Pentecost. A time set aside by God for His people Israel to observe as appointed Feasts in their spiritual calendar and the two Feasts were connected in that, the people were also instructed to count the days in between which gave a total of forty-nine, (Lev:23:15-22.)

After God gave this instruction to Moses the concluding verse says;

> *"When you reap the harvest of your land, do not reap to the very edges of your field or gather the gleanings of your harvest. Leave them for the poor and the alien. I am the LORD your God."*

This is the heart of a compassionate God making provision for the weak and vulnerable and also laying down a foundation for His people regarding their responsibility and care for the disadvantaged in society. In other words, God's people were to live out His teaching beyond the letter of the law, in a fashion which displayed His glory in their own lives by showing His love in their actions.

God spoke these words to Moses about four hundred years before Ruth was even born and it is because of this very instruction Ruth would spend seven weeks during the barley and wheat harvests working in the fields in order to support herself and Naomi.

The seven weeks pass by so quickly and so much happens it's difficult even for us as we read to hold on and wait for the next episode. What must it have been like for Naomi as she waits each day for the door to open and sees Ruth with a smile on her face and her hands filled with food? Her response is surely praise and thanksgiving because God has indeed provided once again food for His people in Bethlehem – the House of Bread, not only that, but He is delivering it to her own front door! Yes, they have much to sing and praise God for.

Heavenly Father, Thank-you for Your Word which reminds us that You have already laid the foundations necessary for us to live out our lives showing Your grace and mercy to others.

Thank-you also that You are waiting for us with the answer to our prayers because You have seen beforehand those things which enter our lives and leave us bereft and wanting, and in Your foreknowledge have already made provision.

Forgive us when we think you are distant and absent, may our focus be to acknowledge Your hand in all that happens in our lives so that we can enjoy the moments of surprise when You come in unexpected ways and that we can once again lift our hearts and voices in praise and thanksgiving.

Blessed are those whose strength is in you,
who have set their hearts on pilgrimage.
As they pass through the Valley of Baca,
(weeping)
they make it a place of springs;
the autumn rains also cover it with pools.
For the LORD God is a sun and shield;
the LORD bestows favour and honour;
no good thing does he withhold from
those whose walk is blameless.
O LORD Almighty, blessed is the man who
trusts in you.

Psalm 84:5-6;11-12.

Isaiah 60:1-2b
"Arise, shine, for your light has come, and the glory of the LORD rises upon you.
...but the LORD rises upon you and his glory appears over you.

It's springtime in Bethlehem, the season of new beginnings, new birth, fresh vigour. A time which brings with it a sense of 'throwing off' as it were the dark blanket of winter and reaching out to embrace the light refreshment of a new season. For Naomi and Ruth their 'winter season' has been long and dreary and filled with sadness on many levels. Now they were starting afresh and whatever lay ahead of them they would face it together as one. Ruth had pledged herself to caring for her mother-in-law and Naomi was adjusting to this faithfulness and learning to live with a daughter for the very first time. The journey they had just shared together took true grit on behalf of them both. Naomi had seen in Ruth a woman of strength, purpose and determination and Ruth had witnessed a needy child of God in Naomi.

God in His infinite grace and mercy had brought these two women together each with their own individual needs and also with their individual personalities which created a bond between them complementing their relationship. One couldn't do without the other; together they were a team.

Back living in Bethlehem meant they had to support themselves and seek to survive. As they were two barren women as well as being widows the sense of animosity would be palpable. Not having husbands or sons to support them took away their status in the community and set them on a sure road to poverty.

The Bible gives many examples of what it meant to be barren in their society. Not producing a son to carry on the husband's name could mean another wife being taken, as is the case in the story of Hanna (1Sam.1);

> She was mocked and made fun of by the other wife
> wept and would not eat
> was downcast
> is described as being in bitterness of soul
> full of misery
> deeply troubled
> in great anguish and grief.

Hanna poured out her soul to God in prayer and in her pleading with God for a child, she prayed desperately for a son.

In the new testament we read of Elizabeth who was barren and passed child bearing age. She along with her husband Zecharias prayed for years for a child. The LORD blessed them with a son. When she became pregnant with her son Elizabeth said, "In these days he has shown his favour and taken away my disgrace from among the people (Luke1:25b)

These examples give us a picture of the stress and anxiety suffered by women who were barren in a male dominated society and it is into this society the young Moabitess comes. It would take great strength of character for her not only in her barrenness and widowhood, but also as a foreigner, to step outside the house of Naomi and make her way to the fields of Bethlehem. Once again it is to stay alive and escape death, Naomi gives permission for Ruth to go and glean.

As she steps out into the spring sunshine, in her heart Ruth is trusting the God of Israel for her future and what a future it turns out to be! Unknown to her she is about to set her name firmly into the ancestry of the Lord Jesus Christ.

Heavenly Father, only You can turn our winters into spring because You are the Great Creator, the One who renews, refreshes, restores and replenishes our barren souls in the sunshine of Your love.

> **Will You not revive us again, that your people may rejoice in You?**
> **Ps.85:6**

Therefore, remember that <u>formerly</u> you who
are Gentiles by birth and called 'uncircumcised'
by those who call themselves 'the circumci-
sion' (that done in the body by the hands of
men) remember that at that time you were -
separate from Christ excluded from citi-
zenship in Israel and foreigners to the cov-
enants of the promise without hope and
without God in the world.

<u>But now</u> in Christ Jesus you who were once
far away <u>have been brought near</u> through
the blood of Christ. For he himself is our
peace...
<u>consequently</u>,
you are no longer foreigners and aliens
<u>but</u>
fellow-citizens with God's people
<u>and</u>
members of God's household.
        Ephesians 2:11-14,19

Ruth 2:3
.....as it turned out, she found herself
working in a field belonging to Boaz...

As Ruth leaves the house that first morning her task for the day is to glean enough from the fields which would feed her and her mother-in-law that evening and sustain them through to the next day when she would do it all over again. This was going to be a day by day existence for these two widows and Ruth was the one able enough physically to do this back-breaking work in the heat of the day, each and every day, during harvest time. Her first day would be a real test of endurance both mentally and physically but this was a woman with a deep sense of God's goodness to His people and she would be working with that in mind. Ruth was about to carry out a task which God Himself had set aside for people in her position: the widow, the stranger and the poor and as she fitted into each of these categories she had the faith to believe God would deliver in providing for her and Naomi.

On that same morning someone else steps out to go to the fields. His name is Boaz, another of the 'men of Bethlehem.' Here is a man who is about to play a major role in the purposes of God concerning Ruth and Naomi and the furtherance of His great plan of salvation. A man who is described in terms of wealth and position. When we meet Boaz later, we see someone who also loved God and sought to live his life on Godly principles.

On their walk through Bethlehem that morning neither one had any idea that the covenant God -YAHWEH- was graciously bringing them to a chosen moment which would change their lives forever. Boaz the wealthy landowner and Ruth, the barren widow certainly gives us a taste for a good romantic novel but in the plans and purposes of God, this meeting would have implications far beyond the scope of any of our fantasies or our imaginations. For one of them the walk to the field is for the purpose of staying alive, for the other, it's an opportunity to drop in on the employees and see how business is today. Practical, ordinary and common purposes which will soon become extraordinary and uncommon purposes.

The fields around Bethlehem were now full and rich with the LORD's provision. There was no need to sign up with any authority in order to go and glean. Any and all who fitted the category for the purposes of gleaning relied upon the instruction given by God to His people and on the kindness of the farmer or landowner to fulfil their obligation to this instruction. Ruth was there on God's authority.

Ruth made her way to one of the fields and v.3 tells us, *'as it turned out, she found herself working in a field belonging to Boaz, who was from the clan of Elimelech.'* She had no agenda that day other than glean but with God in control of all her circumstances, His agenda led her to the field of Boaz. God had His man waiting in the wings to welcome Ruth fully into that place of hope; hope which has been burning within her since it first began on the road to Bethlehem. This hope which had been growing will soon find it's resting place. The rewards of her faith and obedience will be found in the fields of Bethlehem, through a 'man of Bethlehem' in the place known as, 'The House of Bread.'

What a day this will be!

Father God, as we read these verses and see your guiding hand in the circumstances of Ruth, our hearts rejoice in wonder and praise. With a faith in you which is still being cultivated she moves through the pages of history showing us how we can follow after You in a simple and uncomplicated fashion. May our hearts 'burn within us' as happened with the disciples on the road and also with Ruth. May the journey along life's pathway be one which looks up and away from the circumstances and looks by faith to the One who wants to lead and guide us into rich pastures.

He makes me lie down in green pastures, he leads me beside quiet waters, he restores my soul. Ps. 23.2

As the Scripture says, "Anyone who trusts in him will never be put to shame." For there is no difference between Jew and Gentile - the same Lord is Lord of all and richly blesses all who call on him, for,

"Everyone who calls on the name of the Lord will be saved."

How, then, can they call on the one they have not believed in?

And how can they believe in the one of whom they have not heard?

And how can they hear without someone preaching to them?

And how can they preach unless they are sent?

As it is written, "How beautiful are the feet of those who bring good news!"

Romans Ch.10;11-15

Joshua 2:1, 6:25
Then Joshua son of Nun secretly sent two spies from Shittim. "Go, look over the land," he said, "especially Jerico," So they went and entered the house of a prostitute named Rahab and stayed there.
But Joshua spared Rahab the prostitute, with her family and all who belonged to her, because she hid the men Joshua had sent as spies to Jerico - and she lives among the Israelites to this day.

The story of Rahab is a fascinating account of a Gentile woman who was rescued from death and destruction by the advancing Israelites as they entered the promised land. She lived in the city of Jerico the first city to be taken. When spies were sent into Jerico it was to the house of Rahab they came and while there she protected them from the King of Jerico by hiding them under stalks of flax on her rooftop. She did this because she, as well as everybody else in Jerico had <u>heard</u> of the God of the Israelites and she decided to put her trust in Israel's God. In effect, she risked her own life by hiding the spies and allowing them to continue with their re-connaissance mission, but this was a price she was willing to pay in order to experience for herself a life lived under the true God of Heaven.

Israel's God had parted the Red Sea and defeated Kings! The false gods of Jerico were but idols of wood and stone, powerless and useless compared to this God. The false gods she worshipped couldn't do these things so she made a decision and her statement of faith would have greatly encouraged the two spies,

"I know that the LORD has given this land to you
and that a great fear of you has fallen on us
so that all who live in this country are melting in fear because of you...
...the LORD your God is God in heaven above
and on the earth below..."

Rahab knew there was no point in standing against a power such as this and she believed what she had <u>heard</u> not only for herself but for her family also and she was bold enough to make a request in return for her kindness;

"Now then, please swear to me by the LORD...that you will spare the lives of my father and mother, my brothers and sisters, and all who belong to them, and that you will save us from death."

Her request was received by the two men and they made a promise to her by swearing on oath, deliverance for her and her whole family provided she brought them into her house and hung a scarlet rope from the window when the city would be taken. I imagine she hung out the scarlet rope as soon as they left just to make sure she wouldn't forget! I can also see her running around Jerico gathering up her family and letting them into the secret. This Gentile woman believed she would be delivered from death and she wasn't disappointed (Ch.6:25).

What a story this young woman had to tell to her beloved son Boaz as he grew up in Bethlehem. (It is presumed her husband Salmon was one of the spies.) Here was a woman just like Ruth who was an 'outsider' in more ways than one.

The rich landowner from Bethlehem knew exactly how a woman felt when she was a foreigner and an alien. He also knew how she felt when she acknowledged the covenant God of Israel and experienced for herself

His bountiful blessings. He knew, because he had <u>heard</u> from the lips of his own mother - Rahab the prostitute:

A woman brought by the Grace and Mercy of a compassionate God into the family of His chosen people.

A woman who never forgot His goodness and who passed on to her son what kind of man he could be as he too shared in these blessings.

A woman whose name is also recorded in the lineage of Jesus our Saviour (Matt.Ch.1).

When Naomi told this story as she and Ruth set out across the Jordan, neither of them knew then that the son of Rahab would turn out to be their deliverer and redeemer.

God had His 'man of Bethlehem' waiting to welcome Ruth and Naomi into the

'House of Bread'

Your Father knows what you need
before you ask him.
Matthew 6:8

Ask and will be given to you;
seek and you will find;
knock and the door will be opened to you.
For everyone who asks receives:
he who seeks finds:
and to him who knocks,
the door will be opened.
Matthew 7:7-8

Ask and you will receive,
and your joy will be complete.
John 16:24

Now to him who is able to do immeasurably
more than all we ask or imagine....
Ephesians 3:20

Ruth 2:7
"Please let me glean among the harvest-ers"

For most people the first day at school or work is a day filled with all sorts of emotions. Walking into unfamiliar surroundings filled with unfamiliar people to engage in unfamiliar activities causes stomachs to churn, legs to tremble and prompts a general feeling of anxiety and apprehension. On her first day perhaps Ruth could have identified with such feelings.

Going to the fields that morning was a matter of life and death, she was on a personal rescue mission, Ruth had already pledged allegiance to Naomi and she wasn't going to go back on her promises. Her intentions of faithfulness to her mother-in-law were honourable and Ruth was now taking responsibility to provide for them both. Her hope lay in the LORD's instruction to His people to leave part of the harvest for the gleaners and she believed His word, was acting upon it and trusted the farmer who owned the field, would do likewise.

When she arrived at the field she approached the foreman and requested to 'glean and gather among the sheaves behind the harvesters'. Ruth didn't need to ask permission to glean but she went a step beyond what the Law had already given her permission to do because she was asking to work where the gleaners were not allowed to work, she was asking to work behind the harvesters!

The usual procedure in harvesting was that the hired men went into the field first and with one hand they grabbed the stalks of grain, with the sickle in the other hand they cut the stalks off at the base and then laid the stalks on the ground. Next came the women who would gather the cut stalks and bind them into bundles which would then be taken to the threshing floor where the raw kernels of grain were separated from the husks. The gleaners were last to come into the field but only after those who went before them had finished their jobs of cutting, binding and removing the stalks from the field.

Ruth could see that what was left after this operation was meagre and wouldn't possibly be enough to feed two people. It would take hours of hard work and there would be very little to show for it all in the end, so she boldly approached the foreman and presented him with her request. She took a great risk in asking to do this because it left her open to criticism and possible verbal abuse from other gleaners. On the other hand, they may have given her a fool's pardon in that she was a stranger and foreigner who wasn't aware of the procedure. Whichever way it was, Ruth wanted to make sure she brought home good grain and enough of it.

The foreman of course, wouldn't have the authority to grant permission for her to gather among the sheaves behind the harvesters and so she goes and takes her place amongst the gleaners.

We have already noticed that Ruth is not someone who accepts the status quo, but a woman who moves forward after giving much thought to the knowledge she had accumulated from Naomi who had given her plenty of information about gleaning. They probably even sat and discussed if there was some other way in which they could generate funds to support themselves as gleaning was a very strenuous and tiring occupation, nevertheless it seemed this was the way to go but Ruth being the woman she was, wasn't going to settle for anything less than a good reward for a good day's gleaning and she purposes to make the most of what was available. In asking to glean among the sheaves she is suggesting that not only should gleaners be given opportunity under the requirements of the Law to glean, but that the landowner should stretch his generosity beyond the 'crumbs' and give them a 'loaf'! This was a bold and courageous act on behalf of a woman who was a foreigner in Bethlehem and it reminds me very much of the faith of the Canaanite woman in Matthews gospel which we will look at in our next reading.

Heavenly Father, there can be times when we resign ourselves to the status quo and the courage to make or cause change seems too sacrificial. The fear of failure, rejection or the sting of rebuff keeps us from stretching our wings and soaring with You.
Help us to realize that in our own strength we have limited power but in Your strength the impossible becomes the possible.

*Let us therefore come **boldly** unto the throne of grace, that we may obtain mercy, and find grace to help in time of need.*
Hebrews 4:16

Leaving that place, Jesus withdrew to the region of Tyre and Sidon. A Canaanite woman from that vicinity came to him, crying out, "Lord, Son of David, have mercy on me! My daughter is suffering terribly from demon-possession,"

Jesus did not answer a word.

So his disciples came to him and urged him "Send her away, for she keeps crying out after us."

He answered, "I was sent only to the lost sheep of Israel."

The woman came and knelt before him, "Lord, help me!" she said.

He replied, "It is not right to take the children's bread and toss it to their dogs,"

"Yes, Lord," she said, "but even the dogs eat the crumbs that fall from their masters' table."

Then Jesus answered, "Woman, you have great faith! Your request is granted." And her daughter was healed from that very hour.

Matthew 15:21-28

John 6:35
Jesus said "I am the Bread of Life. He who comes to me will never go hungry and he who believes in me will never be thirsty."

We have already seen the boldness of Ruth in that she wasn't going to settle for 'this is the way we've always done it' attitude. With her new found faith in Israel's God she could see there could be more flexibility in the outworking of God's instruction with regard to the farmer and the gleaner and it is in her action we can see a parallel story in the N.T.

Matthews gospel gives us an account of the Canaanite woman approaching Jesus when He came to her region. It is also with a sense of surprise and shock we read of Jesus seemingly ignoring her and even speaking to her in terms which suggest He is putting her in the category of a dog! (Ch.15:21-28.) None of this is correct of course and Jesus and the woman both knew it.

What we see here is Jesus giving His disciples a master class on what it means to reach beyond their 'learned' and 'historic' theories and opinions about the Love, Grace and Mercy of God.

The two words 'Canaanite woman' already give us a clue to the problem as Jesus saw it in His disciples. She was a *foreigner* and a *woman*. The attitude of the disciples was to 'send her away...they couldn't be bothered with her, she was pestering them and anyway, no self-respecting Rabbi would be seen talking to a woman and a Gentile at that.

The question is, "Why was she crying out after them?"

Answer:

She knew that Jesus had healed people,
She needed help,
She had a daughter who was demon-possessed.
<u>She had faith to believe that if she asked him,
Jesus would answer her request.</u>

It looked as if Jesus was just ignoring her when He spoke to the disciples, *"I was sent only to the lost sheep of Israel"* The disciples probably thought Jesus wanted rid of her too when they heard these words but the woman wasn't put off in the least, <u>she came and knelt before Him and continued to plead for His help.</u>

Once again when Jesus responded to her request for help He spoke not to her but to the disciples! He was not calling her a dog, rather He was expressing in words, what the disciples thought in their heads regarding Gentiles and how they were viewed - they were no better than dogs.

The language of Jesus is very strong and for the woman very insulting, but Jesus is drawing the disciples out of **their** comfort zone and in a sense suggesting to them, *"How can you sit there and watch this broken, pleading woman and allow your prejudices against women and Gentiles restrict the Love, Grace and Mercy of God found in me?"*

He was in fact throwing her a life-line and she grabbed it with both hands by saying, *"But even the dogs eat the crumbs..."*

Then Jesus spoke **to her**, *"Woman, you have great faith! Your request is granted"*

This woman had heard what Jesus could do and nothing was going to prevent her from approaching him and seeking His help and healing for her daughter, regardless of any cultural, social, religious, political rules or regulations.

Her daughter was held in the grip of the *evil one* and

she was pushing the boundaries aside and looking to Jesus and *Him only* as the answer to her prayer and she wasn't disappointed.

The Canaanite woman received not only the *'crumbs'* but the whole *'loaf'*.

Our Father in heaven,
hallowed be your name,
your kingdom come, your will be done
on earth as it is in heaven.
*Give us today our **daily bread**.*
Forgive us our debts,
as we also have forgiven our debtors.
And lead us not into temptation,
*but deliver us from the **evil one***
Matthew 6: 9-13

The LORD said to Moses, "Tell Aaron and his sons, this is how you are to bless the Israelites. Say to them:
The LORD bless you and keep you;
the LORD make his face shine upon you and be gracious to you;
the LORD turn his face towards you and give you peace."

"So they will put my name on the Israelites, and I will bless them."
Numbers Ch.6:22-27

Ruth 2:4
"The LORD be with you"... "The LORD bless you"

During the course of the day Boaz, the owner of the field Ruth was working in, arrived. His entrance was one of grace and godliness as he greets the harvesters, *"The LORD be with you!"*

These were the first words Ruth heard from the lips of Boaz - and what words!

The harvesters returned the greeting, *"The LORD bless you!"*

What a wonderful way in which this boss approached his employees! How such a greeting can encourage hearts and remove fears. A boss such as this wouldn't give anyone cause for concern, on the contrary, he would invite communication, partnership and have a growing business.

The main reason Ruth and her mother-in-law came back from Moab was because of what they had heard 'The LORD' was doing in Bethlehem and now she was listening to the voices of those whose delight was in this same 'LORD,' the covenant God of Israel – YAHWEH. She was surrounded by a praising, thankful and generous group of people. As far as Ruth was concerned there was no better place than right here and right now in the field of Boaz,' the man of Bethlehem.'

This young, poor, foreign, widowed, barren woman from Moab had just heard the first tones of the Grace of God in the greeting of Boaz to his workers and the hope which had been kindled in her heart back on the road was now burning like the heat of the mid-day sun.

The hope she had placed in 'The LORD' for her own future
The hope she expected for better things to come
The hope of being favoured by somebody who would allow her to glean
The hope that God would provide for her and Naomi.

She was *filled with hope* which was growing from a trusting faith in 'The LORD.'

What a 'first day' this was turning out to be and Ruth sensed her hope was well founded and that her confident faith was surely going to be rewarded.

Let us remind ourselves this story takes place in the times of the Judges. A time in the history of God's people when '*everyone did as he saw fit*' (Judges21:25) Yet not everyone, it seems, fell into this category. There were those who were still faithful to God's word and because of them, God was blessing and fulfilling His Divine purposes through them. Boaz was included in this number. He was a man who loved God and sought to live his life according to God's precepts.

Heavenly Father, our world to-day isn't much different from that of the times of the Judges.
May we stay faithful and obedient so that others may be blessed because of our hope in You.
Help us to encourage and spur one another on as we wait for Your appearing.
Strengthen our hearts as we seek to defend and uphold Your precepts.
As You bless us may we in turn be a blessing to others.

Your ears shall hear a word behind you saying, "This is the way, walk in it" Isaiah 30:21

Arise, LORD!
Lift up your hand, O God.
Do not forget the helpless.
But you, O God,
<u>do see</u> trouble and grief;
<u>you consider</u> it to take it in hand.
<u>You hear</u>, O LORD, the desire of the af-
flicted;
<u>you encourage</u> them
and
<u>you listen</u> to their cry
    Psalm 10:12,14,17

Ruth Ch.2:5
Boaz asked the foreman of his harvesters,
"Whose young woman is that?"

After Boaz greeted his workers he stood and looked around the field and almost immediately noticed the stranger. When he enquired of the foreman who this was, Boaz learned about the Moabitess and that Naomi was her mother-in-law. The foreman told of Ruth's request to glean and gather **among the sheaves** behind the harvesters and also how hard working she was. As soon as he had finished, Boaz went over to where Ruth was working and began to speak directly to her, "**My daughter...**"

In the Gospel of Mark the Lord Jesus, when speaking to the woman who had just been healed from the issue of blood, addressed her by calling her "Daughter." This is the only woman in the Gospels Jesus ever addressed as such and after spending twelve long years with her condition and having suffered rejection on many levels, Jesus knew she needed a word of tenderness and acceptance. By calling her '**Daughter**' He was re-assuring her of her place in the covenant family of God and in the community. This was the reward for a woman who took the risk of reaching out to Jesus when everybody and everything else was against her.

Ruth was a risk taker too. Hadn't she stood on the road with Naomi and declared her faith in the God of Israel even after all she had been through and had watched her mother-in-law go through? She had walked away from the old way of life and risked all by going to Bethlehem with Naomi. This involved being rejected and ostracised, used and abused, forced to live in poverty, being a foreigner and forever known as the Moabite widow. She took the risk because the word of God and the promises of God were her hope for the future.

When Boaz addresses her as '**Daughter**' he is effectively giving her a rightful place among the people of God. He is accepting her as she is and recognising that she has a positive contribution to make. Boaz sees in Ruth a woman of real worth standing before him, someone who has backbone and isn't afraid to suggest change.

To her, gleaning was more than allowing the poor and the alien to gather up the scraps. She expected the land owner to leave enough so that she and others like her could go back to their homes with plenty! Boaz liked what he saw and he responded very positively by telling her,

Not to go to another field but to stay where she was.
To follow after his own servant girls.
Whenever she was thirsty to go and get a drink from the water jars.
He gave her the reassurance also that he had instructed the men were not to touch her.

The hopes Ruth had when she left home that morning now moved beyond anything she believed would or could happen and how encouraged she must have felt.

What a start to the first day!

Heavenly Father, Ruth is showing us how to believe and trust in ways which challenge our thinking.
May we too be risk takers in allowing ourselves to see potential beyond the obvious.
Trusting in our God who desires to delight in and bless those who follow after Him and who can change

the obvious far beyond what our human minds will ever be able to comprehend.

Sometimes we need new challenges to add freshness to our often mediocre lives.

Help us to rise up from our slumber and believe You have much more for us, as the ideals we have grown up with or have become complacent about, can rob us of living the abundant life You so desire us to live.

Jesus said, "...I have come that they may have life and have it to the full."
John10:10

I love the LORD for he heard my voice;
he heard my cry for mercy.
Because he has turned his ear to me,
I will call on him as long as I live.
The LORD is gracious and righteous;
our God is full of compassion.
The LORD protects the simple-hearted;
when I was in great need he saved me.
For you O LORD, have
delivered my soul from death,
my eyes from tears,
my feet from stumbling,
that I may walk before the LORD
in the land of the living.
        Psalm 116:1-2:5-6:8-9

Ruth Ch.2:10
At this, she bowed down with her face to the ground.
She exclaimed, "Why have I found such favour in your eyes that you notice me – a foreigner?"

Isn't it often the case when the LORD answers our prayers we are totally taken aback? Ruth, for all her boldness in requesting to glean among the sheaves, is now so overwhelmed by the kindness of Boaz that she bows before him in humility and with a deep sense of undeserved grace. Just a few hours previously she had sought to challenge the thinking behind the law concerning the poor and the alien and Boaz had responded far beyond what she expected. To some extent she had blessed him as much as he is now blessing her as his desire to give above and beyond what the law required shows how far he had moved in his own thinking. The generosity extended by Boaz to Ruth, included protection, safety and refreshment. Ruth cannot understand why she should be so favoured (which is remarkable as she herself asked permission of Naomi to glean *'behind anyone in whose eyes she was favoured'* (v.2)

So she asks *"Why....?"* (v.10.) Boaz answer is probably unexpected as he tells her he has heard of all she has done for her mother-in-law since the death of her own husband (v.11.)

This is the first we are made aware of Ruth's own loss. So far the deaths of the men have been focused around Naomi and even though there have been glimpses of what Ruth went through, we now see someone actually acknowledging her own personal grief.

Even Ruth reacts to his mention of her loss when she tells Boaz that he has given her comfort (13.)

She had set aside her own needs to care and provide for Naomi throughout all the sad events which have happened.

Boaz continued to speak of all he had heard about her family and homeland and how she had left all to follow after the God of Israel and stay with Naomi as her daughter. All of these added up to great sacrifices in the life of this young woman and Boaz was not holding back in letting her know that what she had already done and continues to do, deserves credit and is above and beyond what would ever be expected from a daughter-in-law. In a sense he is quite taken with this young woman and he prays over her,

> "May the LORD repay you for what you have done. May you be richly rewarded by the LORD, the God of Israel under whose wings you have come to take refuge."

When Boaz prayed that Ruth would experience the blessing of God for the **kindness** she had shown to Naomi, little did he realize that he would be the answer to his own prayer!

Ruth's first 'public' prayer meeting took place on the road from Moab and now another takes place in a field! On both occasions she was being commended for her **kindness**.

The contrast between these two people couldn't have been greater and yet there is a sense of tenderness and respect as Boaz, in his attitude towards Ruth, displays compassion and grace and she, in her response to him humbly accepts that grace.

What a day, and it's not even mid-morning!

Gracious Father, as Ruth bows in humble thanksgiving at the feet of Boaz, we too, bow in adoration before You because You never cease to amaze us as You pour out Your blessings into our lives, in ways we would never expect, through people we would never expect in circumstances we would never expect.

> **Praise be to the God and Father of our Lord Jesus Christ, who has blessed us in the heavenly realms with every spiritual blessing in Christ.**
> **Ephesians 1:3**

You are the salt of the earth.
But if the salt loses its saltiness,
how can it be made salty again?
It is no longer good for anything,
except to be thrown out and trampled by
men.
You are the light of the world.
A city on a hill cannot be hidden.
Neither do people light a
lamp and put it under a bowl.
Instead they put it on a stand, and it gives
its light to everyone in the house.
In the same way.
Let your light shine before men,
that they may see your good deeds and
praise your Father in heaven.
        Matt. 5:13-16

Ruth 2:12
*"May the L*ORD* repay you....*
"May you be richly rewarded...."

The prayer of Boaz over Ruth comes from the knowledge of all he has heard about her. Ruth had been the talk of the town since she arrived and for all the right reasons. Her entrance unto the Bethlehem scene had impacted the townsfolk both male and female, (we shall see more of this later.) No doubt Naomi had been sharing with her neighbours and friends just how strong and loyal her daughter-in-law was and how her faith in YAHWEH was so childlike and trusting, yet fresh and challenging.

In the sacrifices she had made for her mother-in-law, Ruth had already shown what kind of a woman she was and that her intentions were to be an advocate for Naomi and a voice for the widow. Ruth was determined to seek ways in which she and Naomi could live purposeful, fruitful and meaningful lives as they sought to build up their home.

The man or woman doing 'good things' for the sake of doing them and seeking to be seen or highly thought of will not impress God. Boaz knows that God takes notice of faithful, loving and committed people who give selflessly to others without seeking glory, popularity, financial or material reward for themselves.

The prayer he offered for Ruth came from deep within the heart of a man who knew his God. One who had seen YAHWEH'S faithfulness and love towards His people when at times they didn't deserve it. He knew God had allowed the enemy and famine to come when disobedience entered the lives of His chosen ones in order that He might draw them back to Himself. His knowledge of the Almighty had been learned in living through tough situations and His own close walk with God developed as he observed the acts of God in the lives of His own called out people.

Having heard all about the Moabitess, he now stood before Ruth and saw for himself a woman who had grasped hold of this same God because she had been through the crucible of suffering and had witnessed for herself how precious He was even in the midst of much pain, sorrow and loss.

Without all the teaching and knowledge of a Hebrew upbringing here was a woman who was not going to let go of her steadfast faith. A faith which fully believed that obedience brought blessing.

Boaz was in no doubt God would indeed repay and richly reward her.

The reward Boaz was talking about of course, was that Ruth would go on to experience a deeper relationship with God and that He would be pleased to lead her on with Himself, rewarding her richly as she journeyed with Him and that He would 'repay her for all the years the locusts have eaten,'(Joel 2:25)

Yet again Ruth must have been so encouraged as she listened to such wonderful words from the lips of a total stranger who had been so moved by her actions and purposes. We can almost sense his desire to see her lifted above and away from the dire circumstances she has found herself in and move on to live a rich, rewarding life with the God of Israel, **under whose wings she has come to take refuge.**

Heavenly Father, the world looks at trouble and shakes its fist at You with words of blame and condemnation. Your people look at trouble and see You standing in the midst. Yes, there are questions and times of frustration which cause us to wonder why..... Yet in the knowledge of Your Love, we rest our case and learn to lean on the faithfulness of our Sovereign God, who sees and knows and has already planned the bigger picture for our lives. Help us to take refuge under Your wings when trouble surrounds and threatens.

Whatever you do, work at it with all your heart, as working for the Lord, not for men, since you know that you will receive an inheritance from the Lord as a reward.
Colossians 3:23,24.

The LORD said to Moses,
"Speak to the Israelites and say to them:
 Throughout the generations to come you
are to make tassels on the corners of your
garments, with a blue cord on each tassel.
You will have these tassels to look at and
so you will remember all the commands of
the LORD..."

     Numbers 15:37,39a

He who dwells in the shelter of the Most
High will rest in the shadow of the Almighty.
He will cover you with his feathers
and under his wings you will find refuge.

     Ps. 91:1,4

Ruth 2:12

"...under whose wings you have come to take refuge"

In order for us to fully understand what Boaz meant when he spoke these words, we need to briefly acquaint ourselves with one of the instructions God gave the Hebrews, (Num.15:37-41)

God's people were to make **tassels** on the corners of their garments so that they would *'remember all the commands of the LORD.'* These tassels were to be a **visible** reminder of God's holiness and the requirement to obey His commands.

The Hebrew word for the **corner** of this garment also means **'wing.'**

It was a rectangular, four-cornered garment with an opening in the centre for the head to go through and was called a **Tallit** and would have been worn as an outer garment.

Because the **corners** (wings) represented the Word of God, the wearer was in effect *covered* with and *surrounded* by the Word of God as well as publicly displaying the importance of God's commandments in the life of His people.

They were *'wrapped'* and *clothed* in His Word and this was the place of *shelter, safety* and *protection.*

If the wearer of the **Tallit** raised both arms sideways, the picture of being **'under His wings'** became apparent.

As the tassels represented the Word of God, we can now begin to understand more fully the account of the woman with the issue of blood who came up behind Jesus and touched the hem of his garment, (Mark.5:25-34.) What she did was not something out of the ordinary in that time and culture. The rabbi's of the day would have been used with the 'common' people touching their clothing because it displayed the Word of God and folk would reach out in faith believing that God would have mercy on them in whatever they were praying for. There would have been a sense that these garments were somewhat 'sacred' and the woman in Marks gospel would have been aware of this 'visual aid' concerning the commands of God. When she reached out and grasped the hem **(tassel)** of Rabbi Jesus' garment, she was by faith taking <u>hold</u> of God and His Word and placing herself **'under His wings'** with the complete assurance that He would meet her need in that place of safety, security and protection. Her faith was in the <u>Word of God</u>, **not** *the tassels,* **they** were only a representation of that Word.

The **tassels** also included coming *'in under'* the blessing of the covenant and so, creeping up behind Him, as low to the ground as she could go and believing for healing, she reached out and touched the hem **(tassel)** of His garment, the representation of God's Word and she wasn't disappointed. Healing came immediately! The peace and blessing of the covenant was pronounced upon her as Jesus declared,

"**Daughter**, your faith has healed you. Go in (*into*) peace"

For someone who hadn't known peace for twelve years, this was truly a wonderful blessing. She was being assured of the covenant promises of God to His people because she had by faith, **placed herself** *'under His* *wings.'* When Boaz prayed over Ruth "**...under whose wings you have come to take refuge**," the word for *wings* in this prayer is the same word for corner, referring to the place where the tassels hung, perhaps even on the garment he was wearing as a Hebrew child of God!

She had come to faith in the God of Israel and by so doing she too, like the woman with the issue of blood, had **placed herself** *'under His wings'* and was therefore included amongst His covenant people and would benefit from His peace and His blessing.

Praise the LORD
Blessed is the man who fears the LORD,
who finds great delight in his commands.
His children will be mighty in the land;
the generation of the upright will be blessed.
Wealth and riches are in his house,
and his righteousness endures forever.
Even in the darkness light dawns for the
upright,
for the gracious and compassionate man.
Good will come to him who is generous
and lends freely,
who conducts his affairs with justice.
Surely he will never be shaken;
a righteous man will be remembered forever.
He will have no fear of bad news;
his heart is steadfast, trusting in the LORD.
His heart is secure, he will have no fear;
in the end he will look in triumph on his foes.
He has scattered abroad his gifts to the
poor,
his righteousness endures forever,
his horn will be lifted high in honour.
The wicked man will see and be vexed,
he will gnash his teeth and waste away;
the longings of the wicked will come to
nothing.
          Psalm 112

Ruth Ch.2:14
At mealtime Boaz said to her,
"Come over here. Have some bread and
dip it in the wine vinegar."

Ruth had already been gleaning for several hours and probably pre-occupied with thoughts concerning the generosity of Boaz and how she had been shown such favour and kindness both on a material and emotional level.

She had found her song again in a field in Bethlehem and she was singing, if not audibly, most definitely, within her heart.

Centuries later in these same fields angels would be singing and praising,

"Glory to God in the highest, and on earth
peace to men on whom his favour rests"
Luke Ch2:14

Ruth's hope for a new beginning was certainly getting off to a good start and she probably couldn't wait to get home and tell Naomi all that had happened.

As she worked Ruth heard her name being called. She looked up and saw Boaz beckoning to her.

"Come over here...."

He was inviting her to lunch!
Ruth took her place among the harvesters and Boaz

himself offered her some roasted grain. She ate all she wanted and had some left over which she stored away so that she could take it home to Naomi.

Boaz had extended his generosity yet again to this young foreign widow from Moab and Ruth was very grateful, not only to him, but also to the God of Israel who was showing His kindness and faithfulness to the poor, the widow and the alien through this man of Bethlehem.

Earlier she had asked, *"**Why** have I found such **favour** in your eyes that you notice me – a foreigner?"*

Later she said, *"**May I continue** to find **favour** in your eyes, my lord."*

Now, she is confused and excited at the same time.

What a day it has been for Ruth so far and it's not over yet......

Heavenly Father, I am reminded of the invitation of Jesus who wants to give us rest from all those things which weigh us down and cause grief and sorrow.
Because of His Grace and favour He bids us 'come' and lay it all at his feet.
Whatever it is we are carrying, whether it be a broken relationship, unemployment, financial problems or illness, it matters not.
He wants us to come to Him and be fed from His own hand, the food of His precious Word. When we come into His Presence we discover there is fullness of joy. (Ps.16:11)
May we respond to His invitation with broken and contrite hearts and find in Him the answer to all our needs.

"Come to me, all you who are weary and burdened, and I will give you rest." Matt.11:28

What good is it, my brothers, if a man
claims to have faith but has no deeds?
Can such faith save him?
Suppose a brother or sister is without
clothes and daily food.
If one of you says to him, "Go, I wish you
well; keep warm and well fed,"
but does nothing about his physical needs,
what good is it?
In the same way, faith by itself,
if it is not accompanied by action,
is dead.

James 2:14-17

Ruth Ch.2:15
As she got up to glean, Boaz gave orders to his men....

Rested, refreshed and well fed, Ruth began her work for the afternoon unaware of the conversation going on in the background between Boaz and the harvesters,

"even if she gathers among the sheaves, don't embarrass her. Rather, pull out some stalks for her from the bundles leave them for her to pick up and don't rebuke her" (vs.15-16)

Boaz is operating now in a fashion way beyond what the Law required and I'm sure even his workers wondered at such *kindness*. Nevertheless, the boss had spoken and Ruth would now be in the position she had requested of the foreman when she entered the field that morning. She would *glean among the harvesters.*

Not only that but they were to pull out stalks for her to pick up!

How excited she must have been when the foreman came and gave her this news.

Ruth had been hoping and trusting for a good day's gleaning but this was more than she had thought possible.

In the Hebrew, the word for kindness is *hesed*. This is

a word which is the centre piece of the relationship between YAHWEH and His covenant people. It is descriptive of the steadfast love and faithfulness shown by God to His chosen people who in turn ought to reveal these characteristics in their own lives one towards another.

The book of Ruth sings with *hesed*. We found it in the first chapter, when Naomi commended both her daughters-in-law for their **kindness** towards her and each of their husbands and prayed that they in turn would know and experience for themselves the **kindness** of the LORD.

There is no doubt that Ruth was full of hesed, this selfless love which she gives to Naomi without any sign of moaning or complaining.

Now it's the turn of Boaz to display *hesed* not only towards Ruth but also to Naomi.

What we see in Boaz is a man who loves God and is displaying in his own life the characteristics of one who is in covenant relationship with YAHWEH. His gracious generosity towards Ruth is coming from an obedient heart to the Word and ways of God.

Here in the story of Ruth we see God's people displaying their faith openly in a practical fashion and it should challenge our own hearts to love beyond limits those who need to see the face, the hands, the feet of God and hear the word of God in the ordinariness of daily living.

The book of James in the New Testament talks about living the life of faith without works. James is saying this kind of faith is useless, it is dead faith. He is not saying we work to gain favour with God, rather we work because the love of God constrains us. It is the outworking of God's work within.

Heavenly Father, help us to put our faith into action in those areas of our lives where we fall short.

It is so easy to pray about other people's needs without realising that we could actually be the answer to some of those needs.

*Boaz prayed that Ruth would be richly rewarded and we see God using him to be the answer to that prayer because he has the means to do so and the **kindness** of God in His heart.*

*May we seek opportunities to richly bless those who may be seeking food, rest and shelter to-day with the same spirit of **kindness** which God has given us.*

As the body without the spirit is dead, so faith without deeds is dead. James 2:26

I waited patiently for the LORD;
he turned to me and heard my cry.
He lifted me out of the slimy pit,
out of the mud and the mire;
he set my feet upon a rock
and gave me a firm place to stand.

He put a new song in my mouth
a hymn of praise to our God.
Many will see and fear
and put their trust in the LORD

Blessed is the man who
makes the LORD his trust,
who does not look to the proud,
to those who turn aside to false gods.

Many, O LORD my GOD,
are the wonders you have done.
The things you planned for us
no-one can recount to you;
were I to speak and tell of them
they would be too many to declare.

Yet I am poor and needy;
may the LORD think of me.
You are my help and my deliverer;
O my God, do not delay.

     Psalm 40:1-5;17

Ruth 2:19
"Blessed be the man who took notice of you"

Evening arrived and Ruth who had been busy all day, was tired. She still had to thresh the barley and bag it to carry it home. The amount she ended up with far exceeded her expectations and it is likely Boaz probably sent one of the men to help her carry it.

Naomi must have spent the day wondering how Ruth was managing and she would have been glad to see Ruth safely home. The sight of the abundance in Ruth's arms, when she arrived home, was so overwhelming and more so when Ruth produced the remainder of her lunchtime meal.

In her excitement Naomi began to question Ruth about the happenings of the day.

"Where did you glean today? Where did you work? Blessed be the man who took notice of you!"

As Ruth gave her mother-in-law a recital of the day's events she mentions the name Boaz.

Even as she speaks his name to Naomi, it's probable that Ruth may have been 'seeing' God in Boaz:

His grace

His kindness

His generosity

His compassion

His concern

His provision

His protection

His acceptance

His comfort....all the attributes of God Ruth had heard from Naomi, as she told her the stories of the God of Israel. Perhaps the parents of Boaz (if both or either were still alive) spoke so much of their Great God that Boaz sought to live up to his high calling to the very best of his ability as one of God's chosen people and it was displayed in his actions. God working in and through Boaz had made a difference in the lives of these two women and as a result Naomi exclaims, *"The LORD bless him!"*

Here we see a woman whose faith in God is fully restored and whose hope in God is renewed. Naomi thought she had come back to Bethlehem 'empty' but she hadn't reckoned on the bountiful blessing God had given her in Ruth the Moabitess. Naomi too, was 'seeing' God again in a fresh new way through this young woman whose heart was fully committed to her and who was willing to take such a lowly job as gleaning with no wages and little reward for her efforts, in order to fulfil the pledge she made back on the road. By choosing to glean, Ruth was living God's plan for both their lives and Naomi's faith was enriched by the exuberance of her daughter-in-laws new found faith.

She was invigorated and also intrigued as Ruth continued with her account and told how Boaz had said she was to stay with his workers until they finished harvesting all the grain

God had begun to show Naomi and Ruth what it meant to have 'The LORD' as a husband by bringing to them Boaz, 'the man of Bethlehem,' through whom He would show His Love, Grace and His Mercy.

This was just the first day and what a day!

Heavenly Father, we too rejoice with Naomi and Ruth as we see You providing for their needs.

One day with You can bring so much blessing into our lives when we put our faith and our hope in Your ability to give Your children 'good things'.

As we seek to live as Your people amongst those who have no hope or have lost hope, may we display our hope and become a blessing to others in their afflictions and distress.

For your Maker is your husband
the LORD Almighty is his name
Isaiah 54:5

"Hear my prayer, O LORD,
listen to my cry for help;
be not deaf to my weeping.
For I dwell with you as an alien,
a stranger, as all my fathers were.
Look away from me,
that I may rejoice again
before I depart and am no more."
    Ps. 39:12-13

Better is one day in your courts
than a thousand elsewhere;
I would rather be a doorkeeper
in the house of my God
than dwell in the tents of the wicked.
For the LORD God is a sun and shield;
the LORD bestows favour and honour;
no good thing does he withhold
from those whose walk is blameless.
O LORD Almighty,
blessed is the man who trusts in you.
    Ps. 84:10-12

Ruth Ch.2:20
"He has not stopped showing his kindness to the living and the dead"

No doubt when Naomi finally went to bed that night, her heart was filled with a mix of emotions. She probably thought back over the past ten years and recounted the losses which had occurred in her family, the pillow wet with tears as she remembered her husband Elimelech and their two boys. What a blessing to have not one but two sons, Naomi had felt so complete, so fulfilled as she and her husband set out to raise their family and enjoy the blessing of God's inheritance in their home and on the land. How happy they were as a family until the famine came and took hold of their lives. Watching her sons cry out for food and sustenance was heart-breaking and to see them getting thinner and more gaunt each day was more than she could bear. Elimelech made the decision to go where they could have food to eat and ride out the famine. Leaving family, friends, home and land they walked away from starvation and death only to meet death full on.

Looking back on it all now, Naomi once again walked the road to Moab in her thoughts, every step just as sad and painful as it was ten years ago. So much had happened in those years Naomi had changed from being a vibrant, young housewife into a grieving mother and widow. The years of hardship had taken its toll on her appearance and in her heart to such an extent she felt the need to call herself Mara as all the 'pleasantness' (Naomi means pleasant) had been taken from her life.

How she would have sorrowed that night as these thoughts brought stinging tears to her eyes and intermingling freely with the joy of God's goodness to her from the lives of Ruth and Boaz.

Naomi would never be able to understand God's dealings in her life but what she was so very sure of right now was that God had not forgotten her.

She was not bereft.

God was still caring for her.

His kindness (hesed) displayed in the 'gleanings' of Ruth.

The grim reaper had visited her home in the past but now, the Lord of the harvest had come, in the person of Boaz bringing deliverance, restoration and remuneration.

YAHWEH, whose steadfast love and faithfulness Naomi had felt eluded her, was now manifested by the rich bounty brought home by her loving daughter-in-law Ruth.

In the other room was the Moabitess. She too, having difficulty getting to sleep because of thoughts so filled with awe and wonder. It has truly been a blessed day. A day in which her prayers were answered above and beyond anything she could have dreamed possible. Her days of grief were now passing and a new day had dawned in her life. God had proven Himself to her and she knew all would be well. Naomi would have plenty to do to-morrow as she sorted out the grain and made arrangements for what would be brought home next. Yes, they were both going to be busy, sleep was necessary now...

Father God, my Husband. Thank-you for to-day.
My heart is filled with songs of praise.
You gave me hope and You have rewarded that hope.
Help me to hold on to Your promises for the future.
Thank-you for Boaz, may our friendship grow and mature.
Thank-you for blessing Naomi and showing her that You have plans for her life too.
Give me strength to glean over the next seven weeks and may each day be filled with Your Grace.
Amen
Ruth.

> **Those who sow in tears will reap with songs of joy. He who goes out weeping, carrying seed to sow, will return with songs of joy, carrying sheaves with him.**
> **Psalm 126:5,6**

Therefore, since we have been justified through faith, we have peace with God, through our Lord Jesus Christ, through whom we have gained access by faith into this grace in which we now stand.
And we rejoice in the hope of the glory of God.
Not only so, but we also rejoice in our sufferings, because we know that suffering produces perseverance; perseverance, character; and character, hope.
And hope does not disappoint us, because God has poured out his love into our hearts by the Holy Spirit, whom he has given us.

Romans Ch.5:1-5

Ruth 2:20
"That man is our close relative; he is one of our kinsman-redeemers"

Chapter two began by introducing us to Boaz as a man of standing and a rich relative of Elimelech. Now at the end of the chapter Naomi realizes Ruth had been working in his field. She probably reckons the generosity of Boaz is because he is a relative and therefore is showing care towards her for that very reason. Naomi would now have to explain to Ruth the law of the 'kinsman redeemer' (Lev. 25:47-55).

As a near relative, Boaz could redeem the family property of Elimelech. The word 'redeem' means 'to buy back' or 'set free.' It is the purchase of a person's property or, liberty through the payment of an agreed price. Not only that but the widow of the deceased went with the property. The kinsman redeemer had to marry her and children from this union would inherit the property and 'keep alive' the name of the deceased.

The role of kinsman redeemer had three requirements;
First, he must be a *near* kinsman, related by birth.
Second, he must be *able to pay* the redemption price.
Third, he must be *willing* to purchase.

Boaz fulfils the first two requirements as he was a near relative and he had the means to pay the price required.
The question remains, was he *willing* to play this role?

It has been obvious so far that he is displaying some affection for Ruth but it is also obvious he does not see himself as the one who holds the **right** of redemption. We need to bear in mind also,that the land belonged to Elimelech and **Naomi** is the widow in question here not Ruth.

Naomi had said to her daughters-in-law on the road, *"I am too old to have a husband"* (Ch.1:12) so there is a distinct problem regarding the law of the kinsman-redeemer in the case of Naomi. However, it seems the custom in the time of Ruth allowed for Ruth to come under this law having been married to Mahlon, the eldest son of Elimelech.

Having heard this, Ruth began to realize the possibility for Naomi to have her husband's name continued in Israel, through her. Even though she did not conceive during her marriage to Mahlon, entering into marriage for the purpose of producing an heir for Elimelech perhaps dampened the spirits of Ruth the barren widow from Moab but she had a steadfast faith in YAHWEH and all she had heard about Him included blessing such women with children. Her faith was in the God of the impossible. Should she have opportunity to go in this direction she would trust that God would bless and honour His own written Word because of her obedience.

Heavenly Father, our sins have left us wanting and under Your wrath.

We too, need to be redeemed and we thank-you for our Blessed Saviour Jesus Christ who fulfilled the requirements to be our Kinsman Redeemer in order that those sins could be forgiven.

He had the <u>right</u> to redeem us having been made in human likeness, (Phil. 2:7)

He had the <u>power</u> to redeem when he paid redemption's price,

"It was not with perishable things such as silver and gold that you were redeemed...but with the precious blood of Jesus Christ..." (1Peter 1:18-19)

He was <u>willing</u> to redeem us.

No one took His life from Him, He laid it down Himself, (Jn.10:18)

RUTH Chapter 3

1 One day Naomi her mother-in-law said to her, "My daughter, should I not try to find a home for you, where you will be well provided for?

2 Is not Boaz, with whose servant girls you have been, a kinsman of ours? Tonight he will be winnowing barley on the threshing floor.

3 Wash and perfume yourself, and put on your best clothes. Then go down to the threshing floor, but don't let him know you are there until he has finished eating and drinking.

4 When he lies down, note the place where he is lying. Then go and uncover his feet and lie down. He will tell you what to do."

5 "I will do whatever you say," Ruth answered.

6 So she went down to the threshing floor and did everything her mother-in-law told her to do.

7 When Boaz had finished eating and drinking and was in good spirits, he went over to lie down at the far end of the grain pile. Ruth approached quietly, uncovered his feet and lay down.

8 In the middle of the night something startled the man, and he turned and discovered a woman lying at his feet.

9 "Who are you?" he asked. "I am your servant Ruth," she said. "Spread the corner of your garment over me, since you are a kinsman-redeemer."

10 "The Lord bless you, my daughter," he replied. "This

kindness is greater than that which you showed earlier: You have not run after the younger men, whether rich or poor.

11 And now, my daughter, don't be afraid. I will do for you all you ask. All my fellow townsmen know that you are a woman of noble character.

12 Although it is true that I am near of kin, there is a kinsman-redeemer nearer than I.

13 Stay here for the night, and in the morning if he wants to redeem, good; let him redeem. But if he is not willing, as surely as the LORD lives I will do it. Lie here until morning."

14 So she lay at his feet until morning, but got up before anyone could be recognized; and he said, "Don't let it be known that a woman came to the threshing floor."

15 He also said, "Bring me the shawl you are wearing and hold it out." When she did so, he poured into it six measures of barley and put it on her. Then he went back to town.

16 When Ruth came to her mother-in-law, Naomi asked, "How did it go, my daughter?" Then she told her everything Boaz had done for her

17 and added, "He gave me these six measures of barley, saying, 'Don't go back to your mother-in-law empty-handed.' "

18 Then Naomi said, "Wait, my daughter, until you find out what happens. For the man will not rest until the matter is settled today."

"Do not let your hearts be troubled.
Trust in God, trust also in me.
In my Father's house are many rooms;
if it were not so, I would have told you.
I am going there to prepare a place for
you.
And if I go and prepare a place for you,
I will come back and take you to be with me
that you also may be where I am.
You know the way to the place where I am
going."
        John 14:1-4

Ruth Ch.3:1
One day Naomi her mother-in-law said to her, "My daughter, should I not try to find a home for you, where you will be well provided for?"

Spring time in Bethlehem has brought sunshine and song into the home and hearts of Naomi and Ruth. On the journey from Moab they would have talked together about getting the house and property cleaned and made habitable once again and how they were going to live from day to day until such times as something would change. Whatever that 'something' was they had no idea. What has been displayed by Ruth is the hope of change in their circumstances. Most of all we cannot overlook the providence of God as seen,

When word reached Naomi in Moab that the LORD had *provided* food again in Bethlehem.

Ruth's coming to *faith* in YAHWEH
The *field* in which Ruth found herself working.
The *care* shown by God for the widow through
the *grace* and *generosity* of Boaz.

The combination of all this has helped bring Naomi back to reality. Her profound grief and sense of emptiness had impacted her spiritually as well as mentally and physically. Where once there seemed only darkness and despair God has given her two very precious people

159

in Ruth and Boaz. Now she too begins to hope for a better future as she sees the windows of heaven opened and the faithfulness of God bringing her comfort, provision and encouragement.

Chapter two ends by telling us that Ruth lived with her mother-in-law. Each day she would return from gleaning in the fields of Boaz bringing good reward for her efforts and most likely something more to tell Naomi about the developing friendship between them.

As Naomi thought on these things, she would remember her responsibilities towards Ruth. It was the usual practice that parents arranged marriages and Naomi felt it was her duty to look for a husband for Ruth. She had suggested to both her daughters-in-law in Moab that they go back to their parents home, find new husbands and begin again.(Ch.1:9) Regardless of this, Naomi knew Ruth deserved a home of her own and a husband to look after her.

As she listened to Ruth's daily reports she reckoned Boaz and Ruth would make a good match and so, she set the wheels in motion.

Heavenly Father, when You bring about a set of circumstances which reveal Your Sovereignty and will for our lives, show us how to respond positively and with courage.

Often we fail to see You working out plans and purposes for us, especially when the situation seems irretrievable.

May we learn to 'see' You even when the way seems impossible and we are looking through misted eyes of grief and sorrow.

Bring us out of the darkness of our spiritual winter into the light of spring and refresh our hearts in the sunshine of Your love.

No longer will they call you Deserted, or name your land Desolate.
*But you will be called Hephizibah, (my delight is in her) and your land Beulah, (married) for the L*ORD *will take delight in you.... Isaiah 62:4*

Jesus said to them, "Take off the grave clothes and let him go."
     John 14:1-4

"Blessed are those who wash their robes, that they may have the right to the tree of life and may go through the gates into the city."
     Rev. 22:14

"Blessed are those who are invited to the wedding supper of the Lamb!"
     Rev. 19:9

Ruth 3:2,3
"To-night he will be winnowing barley on the threshing-floor. Wash and perfume yourself, and put on your best clothes."

Naomi had already expressed her desire to see Ruth married again and living in a home of her own. Having explained the role of the kinsman redeemer she now engaged Ruth in a plan of action.

Aware that Boaz will be at the threshing floor that night she decided this would be a good time to approach him. Under the law this would be a perfectly right and proper thing to do and Naomi needed to plan carefully the steps Ruth should take in order to claim the right of the kinsman redeemer.

Only a few short weeks had passed since Ruth walked into the field of Boaz for the first time and now she was about to approach him with a proposal of marriage!

All the months, perhaps years, of grief over the death of her beloved Mahlon had indeed been truly laid to rest as she prepared herself to step out of the home of Naomi and make her way to the threshing-floor of Boaz, her heart filled once more with the hope of a new beginning.

The Moabitess had all the qualifications necessary in order to claim the right of redemption from one of the richest men in Bethlehem,

She was widowed
She was poor.
She had no sons.

When Ruth travelled the road back to Bethlehem with Naomi they probably discussed the dire straits they were in. She never would have thought that awaiting her in Bethlehem was one who would not only provide food that she might live but also be the one in whom she would find full redemption from the circumstances she found herself in.

The providence of God had yet again allowed for this poverty stricken, barren widow from Moab, to be raised up from the destitution in which she had found herself and experience the richness of a life found in one whose generosity and grace knew no bounds.

In order for her to approach Boaz and state her claim in marriage, Ruth needed to lay aside her widows clothes. Ruth's time of mourning had passed. The dress which defined her status as a widow in society, must now be left off and discarded. It was time for new beginnings, new clothes and a new life. A life in which she would be blessed in a union with Boaz and Naomi her mother-in-law would have Elimelech's name raised once again and recorded in the annals of history.

Ruth was a willing participant in the plan because of her faith in God and her former commitment to Naomi. Her desire to see the name of her father-in-law continued in Israel demanded the leap of faith which she was about to embark upon. She was indeed a woman of great courage, faithfulness and determination.

Our gracious, loving, Heavenly Father, how marvellous it is to see how in ages past You made preparation for man from every level of society.

Whether rich or poor, Your laws and commandments laid down the responsibilities and privileges which could be   embraced by all who sought to obey Your word and follow Your ways.

Our hearts rejoice in the grace offered through Your Son Jesus that in the poverty of our souls we can become rich unto salvation because of His sacrifice for sin on the cross.

For you know the grace of our Lord Jesus Christ,
that though he was rich,
yet for your sakes he became poor,
so that you through his poverty
might become rich. 2Cor.8:9

Therefore, brothers, since we have confidence to enter the Most Holy Place by the blood of Jesus, by a new and living way opened for us through the curtain,
that is, his body, and since we have a great high priest over the house of God, let us draw near to God with a sincere heart in full assurance of faith, having our hearts sprinkled to cleanse us from a guilty conscience and having our bodies washed with pure water. Let us hold unswervingly to the hope we profess, for he who promised is faithful.

Hebrews 10:19-23

Ruth 3:3
***"Then go down to the threshing-floor, but
don't let him know you are there until he
has finished eating and drinking."***

For the first time in a long time Ruth felt like a
woman again. Washed, perfumed and in her best
clothes, she left the house and made her way to the
threshing-floor of Boaz.

It was a wise decision to go as darkness fell because
Ruth's clothing now declared her as someone who was
available for marriage. Had she gone earlier in the day,
she might have been vulnerable to attack or molesta-
tion. Being a foreigner and a woman alone placed her at
the mercy of others.

It is possible Ruth was developing a keen interest in
Boaz as each day passed and therefore her obedience
to Naomi would have come more easily because of her
own feelings towards him.

In the cool of the evening she went unnoticed through
the streets of Bethlehem and found a place to wait until
Boaz and the harvesters had finished their merry-mak-
ing.

The end of harvest was a time of rejoicing and praising God for the provision. It had been an act of faith
and obedience to God which brought about the blessing and everyone was overjoyed at the faithfulness of
YAHWEH. Ruth had come to realize more and more the
reality of the God of Israel as she worked in the fields.

The rich harvest gathered there was even more evidence of the existence of God. The gods of Moab couldn't promise or deliver anything like this! As she waited in the shadows and pondered these things she too, must have quietly rejoiced.

How Ruth had managed to conceal herself is difficult for us to comprehend. She had come onto the threshing-floor with a direct purpose, total faith in God and a down to earth attitude. Her wait would soon be over. She had noted the place where Boaz lay and very quietly, she approached him.

When we consider the planning of Naomi and Ruth regarding the claim on Boaz as kinsman redeemer, we are reminded of the responsibility which is ours as we seek to approach the Heavenly Father.

We need to 'wash' ourselves.
In other words we have to confess our sin and purge our consciences as we come before a holy God.
(Ps.24:3,4)

We need the 'perfume' (anointing.)
We are to be the 'fragrance' of Christ. (2 Cor.2:14-16)

We need to change our clothes.
The people of God have been clothed with the right-eousness of Christ, therefore our lives should display the new creation we are because of His great salvation.
(Isaiah 61:10.)

Heavenly Father, thank-you for Jesus our Saviour and kinsman redeemer who alone has given us the right to approach Your throne with boldness and confidence.
We don't need to wait for any particular moment, we can come to You any time, night or day.
Thank-you for the grace and mercy found in Him who willingly obeyed You and because of this we have redemption in His Name.

How priceless is your unfailing love!
Both high and low among men find refuge in
the shadow of your wings.
    Psalm 36:7

Because you are my help,
I sing in the shadow of your wings..
    Psalm 63:7

.Keep me as the apple of your eye;
hide me in the shadow of your wings.
    Psalm 17:8

Ruth 3:4
"When he lies down, note the place where he is lying. Then go and uncover his feet and lie down.
He will tell you what to do."

Ruth had followed the instructions given to her by Naomi without fear or apprehension. In the dark, on the threshing-floor of Boaz she moved among the sleeping men until she reached the place where Boaz lay. Naomi would not have asked her to go to the threshing-floor if she had thought Ruth was in any danger. The conversations and meals she had with Boaz over the past weeks gave Ruth the confidence she needed to feel comfortable and safe. They were certain Boaz would behave honourably.

Boaz was a man of integrity and grace and one who displayed the characteristics which set the people of God apart. He had already acknowledged the plight of Ruth and Naomi by his generosity towards them and perhaps there were moments in the day, when he looked at Ruth and remembered the law concerning the widow and the kinsman redeemer. Yet he had not put himself forward as the one who would act on their behalf.

Ruth had approached quietly, uncovered his feet and lay down. Startled, he awoke and discovered a woman lying at his feet. When Ruth identified herself she asked him to *'spread the corner of his garment over her as he was a kinsman redeemer.'*

There was nothing immoral in what she did. In this

act, according to Eastern custom, she was only asking for the right to his protection. Later, Boaz spread his garment over her, which symbolized his *willingness* to be her kinsman redeemer (v.13.)

Just a few weeks before, Boaz had remarked how Ruth had come 'under the wings' of the God of Israel for refuge. Perhaps this was a preview of what was now taking place at his own feet.

In using this reference the imagery was that of the tassels which hung from the *corners* of the 'tallit,' (the outer garment worn by Hebrew men) and which represented the word of God. The Hebrew word for *wings* here is the same word used for *corner* as in the corner of the garment worn by Boaz.

In requesting that he spread the *corner* of his garment over her, Ruth was by faith, applying the law to her own situation and acting once again on the authority of the word of God.

Not only had she come 'under the wings' of the God of Israel but now she was seeking refuge 'under the wings' of Boaz also. She was asking for his protection in marriage and the law of God had given her the right to do so. In response to her request, Boaz said,

"The Lord bless you, my daughter."

Thank-you Father for the <u>authority</u> of Your Word which helps us stand fast in the day of temptation.

For the <u>power</u> of that Word which causes the devil to flee.

For the <u>love</u> promised in the Word which tells us You gave Your Only Son to die in our place.

For the <u>forgiveness</u> we have in Jesus the Word.

For the Word of <u>Truth</u> in a world where truth is mixed with error.

For the <u>eternal</u> and <u>everlasting</u> Word.

For the <u>hope</u> we have in the <u>faithfulness</u> of Your Word.

You are all sons of God through faith in Christ Jesus, for all of you who were baptised into Christ have clothed yourselves with Christ.

There is neither Jew nor Greek, slave nor free, male nor female, for you are all one in Christ Jesus.

If you belong to Christ, then you are Abraham's seed, and heirs according to the promise.

Galatians 3:26-29

Ruth 3:10,11
"This kindness is greater than that which you showed earlier. You have not run after the younger men, whether rich or poor. And now, my daughter, don't be afraid, I will do for you all you ask. All my fellow townsmen know that you are a woman of noble character."

Rather than chastening Ruth for her action and request, Boaz blessed her. Once again he mentions her kindness (*hesed*) only this time it is towards him! He is honoured that Ruth has approached him considering he is much older. This is also the third time he has referred to Ruth as 'daughter' suggesting yet again there is an age difference between them.

The response from Boaz was very encouraging and Ruth would have been overjoyed.

"don't be afraid. I will do for you all that you ask."

His promises to fulfil those things she had asked of him gave her of comfort.

Ever since he had first laid eyes on Ruth and had heard about her from others, it seemed he had romantic notions. His problem was his age. All along he probably thought Ruth would have had eyes for younger men and rightly so. Wasn't she a young woman?

Ruth seemed more than happy to have him as a husband. Had that not been the case she would not have gone to the threshing-floor and risked so much only to be turned away.

Boaz now, had every intention of marrying Ruth.

To suggest that there was any kind of untoward behaviour between Boaz and Ruth would be denying the truth of scripture. Boaz is introduced as a man of standing (Ch.2:1.) He was someone of status in his community. He was a rich land-owner and a very respected man of Bethlehem.

The Bible also portrays him as a type of Christ and as such, his character revealed he was indeed a man of integrity.

Ruth showed herself to be a woman of worth. Boaz had already made reference to her kindness and her personal sacrifices. He backed that up by telling her all the men in town knew her to be a woman of noble character. She was someone who had already made an impression on the townsfolk in Bethlehem. Had she been anything other, Boaz would not and could not act as kinsman redeemer.

In His time and in His way, the providence of God has brought these two people together. Their paths have crossed in the fields of Bethlehem because God had plans to fulfil through their lives. They are players on the stage of the greatest story ever told, that of God's wonderful plan of redemption. Both of them living out their faith in their own sphere of life. One through brokenness and poverty, the other in riches and abundance.

Yet, neither poverty or riches are barriers to glorifying God and being the man and woman of God they were meant to be. Both of them are living and moving within the perimeters of the word of God and because of this, God's will is being carried out in their lives and will bring much blessing in the future.

Heavenly Father, Ruth and Boaz are fine examples of how to follow after You.
Their faith in Your word gives them the confidence to move forward in life.
Not doubting or questioning - just trusting.
Not looking back, but pressing on.
Not self-seeking but encouraging one another.
Believing the promises and claiming them.

Submit to one another out of reverence for Christ. Ephesians 5:21

I cried out to God for help;
I cried out to God to hear me.

When I was in distress, I sought the Lord;
at night I stretched out untiring hands
and my soul refused to be comforted.
You kept my eyes from closing;
I was too troubled to speak.
I thought about the former days,
the years of long ago;
I remembered my songs in the night.
My heart mused and my spirit enquired:

"Will the Lord reject forever?
Will he never show his favour again?
Has his unfailing love vanished for ever?
Has his promise failed for all time?
Has God forgotten to be merciful?
Has he in anger withheld his compassion?"

Then I thought, "To this I will appeal: the
years of the right hand of the Most High."

I will remember the deeds of the Lord;
yes, I will remember your miracles of long
ago. I will meditate on all your works
and consider all your mighty deeds.

Your ways, O God, are holy.
What God is so great as our God?
You are the God who performs miracles;
you display your power among the peoples.
Ps. 77:1,2,4-15

Ruth 3:12
"Although it is true that I am near of kin, there is a kinsman redeemer nearer than I."

What a blow these words must have been to Ruth. Surely Naomi must have known this! Was she going to lose Boaz? Ruth's mind was in overdrive.

This is probably the reason Boaz did not offer himself as kinsman redeemer, because he wasn't the nearest kinsman at all! He knew this, obviously Naomi wasn't aware of it.

So far, Ruth had been looking by faith to YAHWEH to lead and guide her. Now there seemed to be an obstacle. She will have to dig deep in order to keep holding on.

In it all, Boaz showed himself to be strong and consoling towards her. He had already made up his mind to marry Ruth and he knew it would work out.

He had also said to Ruth, *"...Don't be afraid. I will do for you all that you ask."* These promises helped keep her hope alive.

The other kinsman had first option in redeeming Elimelech's property if he was willing to do so and Boaz knows he needs to protect himself and Ruth from anything which would stand in the way of the law or jeopardize Naomi's situation. He needed to step aside and allow for the law to play it's part and at the same time continue to be Ruth and Naomi's benefactor regardless of any feelings he had for Ruth.

Boaz invited Ruth to stay for the night rather than send her off in the dark on her own. Reassuringly he told her he would deal with the matter in the morning along with the promise of playing the role of kinsman redeemer himself, should the other man refuse.

Ruth, Boaz and Naomi had most likely spent a very restless if not, sleepless night.

Boaz thinking over what he needed to do first thing in the morning regarding the other kinsman.

Naomi wondering how things had gone for Ruth.

Ruth praying in the stillness, that YAHWEH, in whom she had put her hope and her faith, would act on her behalf and bring Boaz back to the home of Naomi as their kinsman redeemer. She lay at his feet until morning as he suggested. When she arose to go back home, Boaz filled her shawl with a very generous amount of barley for Naomi, confirming once again his care for the two widows(v.17.)

Father God, when all seems lost remind us of Your words of promise,

> **The Lord himself goes before you and will be with you;**
> **he will never leave you nor forsake you.**
> **Do not be afraid; do not be discouraged.**
> **Deut.31:8**

But they that wait upon the L<small>ORD</small>
<u>shall</u> renew their strength;
they <u>shall</u> mount up with wings as eagles,
they <u>shall</u> run, and not be weary; and they
<u>shall</u> walk, and not faint.

   Isaiah 40:31

Ruth 3:18
Then Naomi said, "Wait, my daughter,
until you find out what happens.
For the man will not rest until the matter
is settled today."

The two widows had come back to Bethlehem only a short time ago and so much had happened since their arrival but the prospect of marriage was not something Ruth expected as she was an 'outsider.' Who would want to marry a foreigner and a barren one at that?

The purpose of the kinsman redeemer was that he would father a son who would carry on the name of the widows' dead husband and bearing that in mind reveals the depth of faith Ruth, Naomi and Boaz had.

All three knew the implication of such a union, yet there is no sense of doubt that Ruth would not become a mother! Boaz was well aware she had not conceived in her marriage to Mahlon, yet he promised to become her kinsman redeemer should the other man refuse. Naomi had no grandchildren by either of her son's marriages but was trusting this marriage would produce heirs.

The elders of the town when blessing Boaz also talked about children (Ch.4:12.)

Ruth the risk-taker was trusting in YAHWEH, the God of the impossible.

There was nothing she could do to help the situation. Her hope in God, the promises of Boaz and the support of Naomi would sustain her until she was told the outcome of Boaz' meeting with the other kinsman.

Ruth was learning how to 'wait' in the Presence of the LORD. Finding Him in the day of testing and allowing Him to fill her with renewed hope and trust.

One of the most difficult things for us to do is, 'wait'. As God's children we need to learn how to 'wait' upon the LORD. To sit still and allow Him to perfect that which concerns us. He alone knows the end of our story and there is nothing we need to do except trust Him for the outcome. Sometimes obstacles appear which throw us off balance and cause us to doubt God and His work in our lives. He may allow difficulties and trials to come upon us so that we will mature and grow in Him as we seek to look to Him and not depend on ourselves.

Boaz the man of Bethlehem was in town working on Ruth and Naomi's behalf attending to matters which would impact all three of them in one way or another. He would not rest until the matter was settled that very day.

I am reminded here of Jesus, '*The* Man of Bethlehem' who cried out from the cross on Calvary many centuries later,

"It is finished"

The matter concerning my sinful soul before a
Holy God was dealt with by the shedding of His
Precious Blood
that very day!

Day after day every priest stands and performs his religious duties: again and again he offers the same sacrifices, which can <u>never</u> take away sins.
But when this priest (JESUS) had offered for all time <u>one</u> sacrifice for sins, he <u>sat down</u> at the right hand of God.
Hebrews 10:11,12

Heavenly Father, thank-you that we can rest in You because of our Blessed Saviour Jesus and His work on our behalf.
We can 'sit still' and 'wait' because He has <u>finished</u> the work of Salvation.
We do not need to strive or be anxious as You are in control.

185

RUTH Chapter 4

1 Meanwhile Boaz went up to the town gate and sat there. When the kinsman-redeemer he had mentioned came along, Boaz said, "Come over here, my friend, and sit down." So he went over and sat down.

2 Boaz took ten of the elders of the town and said, "Sit here," and they did so.

3 Then he said to the kinsman-redeemer, "Naomi, who has come back from Moab, is selling the piece of land that belonged to our brother Elimelech.

4 I thought I should bring the matter to your attention and suggest that you buy it in the presence of these seated here and in the presence of the elders of my people. If you will redeem it, do so. But if you will not, tell me, so I will know. For no one has the right to do it except you, and I am next in line." "I will redeem it," he said.

5 Then Boaz said, "On the day you buy the land from Naomi and from Ruth the Moabitess, you acquire the dead man's widow, in order to maintain the name of the dead with his property."

6 At this, the kinsman-redeemer said, "Then I cannot redeem it because I might endanger my own estate. You redeem it yourself. I cannot do it."

7 (Now in earlier times in Israel, for the redemption and transfer of property to become final, one party took off his sandal and gave it to the other. This was the method of legalizing transactions in Israel.)

8 So the kinsman-redeemer said to Boaz, "Buy it yourself." And he removed his sandal.

9 Then Boaz announced to the elders and all the people, "Today you are witnesses that I have bought from Naomi all the property of Elimelech, Kilion and Mahlon.

10 I have also acquired Ruth the Moabitess, Mahlon's widow, as my wife, in order to maintain the name of the dead with his property, so that his name will not disappear from among his family or from the town records. Today you are witnesses!"

11 Then the elders and all those at the gate said, "We are witnesses. May the LORD make the woman who is coming into your home like Rachel and Leah, who together built up the house of Israel. May you have standing in Ephrathah and be famous in Bethlehem.

12 Through the offspring the LORD gives you by this young woman, may your family be like that of Perez, whom Tamar bore to Judah."

13 So Boaz took Ruth and she became his wife. Then he went to her, and the LORD enabled her to conceive, and she gave birth to a son.

14 The women said to Naomi: "Praise be to the LORD, who this day has not left you without a kinsman-redeemer. May he become famous throughout Israel!

15 He will renew your life and sustain you in your old age. For your daughter-in-law, who loves you and who is better to you than seven sons, has given him birth."

16 Then Naomi took the child, laid him in her lap and cared for him.

17 The women living there said, "Naomi has a son." And they named him Obed. He was the father of Jesse, the father of David.

18 This, then, is the family line of Perez: Perez was the father of Hezron,

19 Hezron the father of Ram, Ram the father of

Amminadab,

20 Amminadab the father of Nahshon, Nahshon the father of Salmon,

21 Salmon the father of Boaz, Boaz the father of Obed,

22 Obed the father of Jesse, and Jesse the father of David.

Praise the LORD.
Praise the LORD, O my soul.
I will praise the LORD all my life;
I will sing praise to my God as long as I live.

Blessed is he whose help is the God of
Jacob, whose hope is in the LORD his God,
the Maker of heaven and earth,
the sea and everything in them -
the LORD, who remains faithful for ever.

He upholds the cause of the oppressed
and gives food to the hungry.
The LORD sets prisoners free,
the LORD gives sight to the blind,
the LORD lifts up those who are bowed
down,
the LORD loves the righteous.

The LORD watches over the alien and sus-
tains the fatherless and the widow but he
frustrates the ways of the wicked.

The LORD reigns for ever,
your GOD, O Zion, for all generations.

Praise the LORD.
    Ps. 146

Ruth 4:1
Meanwhile Boaz went up to the town gate and sat there.

The town gate was not only an entrance into town but was also the seat of government, the business centre, the place where property, goods and marriages were transacted and legalised. Everyone regardless of their standing in the community went there to transact all sorts of business. There was always a buzz of activity as locals would gather around to hear and see what was going on.

Boaz was waiting for the other kinsman to walk by so that he could discuss with him a family matter which needed legal sanction. Being the rich landowner he no doubt attracted much interest, which helps us understand how he managed to assemble ten elders who would oversee his business (v.2.)

When Boaz put it to the other kinsman that he had the first option of buying the property from Naomi, the man immediately said he would. Then Boaz informed him that with the purchase came Ruth, the widow of Mahlon.

Had the other kinsman purchased the property it would have cost him financially to do so. He would be taking funds from his existing business to buy. He would then have to work the land and bring it up to standard as presumably, it had been lying idle for ten years. This all cost money which would be fine because eventually it would become profitable and add to his own inheritance.

Taking Ruth as his wife added another dimension to all of this. Should she give birth, everything the kinsman had invested, along with Elimelech's estate, would go to that child.

Weighing his options he decides he doesn't want to endanger his own estate and so, he refused the deal.

Here was a man of Bethlehem who stepped back into the shadows not only because he was thinking on a practical level but also because he had no love or concern in his heart for either Naomi or Ruth the Moabitess.
Earlier we said the kinsman redeemer needed to,
be a near relative
be able to pay the redemption price
be willing to purchase

The other kinsman met the first two requirements. He was a near relative, he was willing to buy property but **he was not willing to redeem.**

Boaz is now in a position to put himself forward as the kinsman redeemer for Elimelech.

**This is the wonderful thing about love
it leaps over all obstacles,
opposes every argument,
and moves on relentlessly
until it possesses the object of its affection
and makes it its own.
(Selwyn Hughes)**

Heavenly Father, thank-you that we have a Saviour who did just that.
One who stands before You to-day interceding on our behalf.

We have this hope as an anchor for the soul, firm and secure.
It enters the inner sanctuary behind the curtain, where Jesus, who went before us, has entered on our behalf.
He has become a high priest forever...
Hebrews 6:19,20

For you know that it was not with perishable things such as silver or gold that you were redeemed from the empty way of life handed down to you from your forefathers, but with the precious blood of Christ, a lamb without blemish or defect.

1 Peter 1:18-19

Ruth 4:8
So the kinsman- redeemer said to Boaz,
"Buy it yourself."
And he removed his sandal.

The transaction at the town gate ended when the kinsman-redeemer removed his sandal and handed it to Boaz. 'Now in earlier times in Israel, for the redemption and transfer of property to become final, one party took off his sandal and gave it to the other. This was the method of legalising transactions in Israel' (v.7.)

Boaz now had the 'right' to not only buy all that belonged to Elimelech, Chilion and Mahlon, but had claim also to Ruth's hand in marriage. He had become her kinsman-redeemer.

The elders and all those at the gate raised their
voices in prayer for Ruth and Boaz,
making mention of Rachel and Leah
'who built up the house of Israel'
of *Ephrathah*,
which was the old name for Bethlehem
and in Hebrew means, *fruitful*
that they would be *famous* in Bethlehem
and their family would be like that of Perez
(vs.11-12)

The prayers of the people of Bethlehem were sincere and loving. Their ancestry was of the utmost importance to them as was their town and the future of the nation of Israel.

This was the nation through whom God would send the Redeemer and Bethlehem would be the place of His choosing (Micah 5:2.)

As Boaz rejoiced in the presence of his neighbours and friends he declared to all they were witnesses to the transaction which had just taken place,

"That of maintaining the name of Elimelech, so that his name would not disappear from among his family or from the town records" (v.10.)

The faithfulness of Ruth towards Naomi and her sacrifice of devotion in seeking to keep the name of Elimelech alive, allowed her to use the law of the kinsman redeemer and choose to act as 'surrogate' on Naomi's behalf. In faith, along with Boaz, she trusted that God would bless their actions.

As the hesed of the God of Israel flowed out of their lives one towards the other and each of them acted within the law of YAHWEH, Boaz, Ruth and Naomi had achieved the will of God.

At the beginning of the Book of Ruth we read of Elimelech who along with his family were Ephrathites from Bethlehem. This was a family who had suffered much and yet, even in that suffering, the providence of God has been very evident.

Heavenly Father, Your ways are beyond our understanding. Even through tears, trials and tribulations, You bring blessing. May we see Your purposes rather than our own goals and desires. Help us to encourage others on the journey by displaying kindness ('hesed') by which Your characteristics are displayed.

But the fruit of the Spirit is Love, joy, peace, patience, kindness, goodness, faithfulness, gentleness, self-control. Against such things there is no law.
Galatians 5:22

"Therefore I am now going to allure her;
I will lead her into the desert and speak tenderly to her.

There I will give her back her vineyards
and will make the Valley of Achor (weeping)
a door of hope.

There she will sing as in the days of her
youth, as in the day she came up out of
Egypt.

"In that day," declares the LORD, you will call
me 'my husband'; you will no longer call me
'my master'.

I will betroth you to me for ever; I will betroth you in righteousness and justice, in love
and compassion. I will betroth you in faithfulness, and you will acknowledge the LORD.
I will plant her for myself in the land; I will
show my love to the one I called 'Not my
loved one'. I will say to those called 'Not my
people',
'You are my people'; and they will say, 'You
are my God'"

Hosea 1:14-16,19-20,23

Ruth 4:13
So Boaz took Ruth and she became his wife.

While Boaz and the townsfolk were celebrating at the town gate, Ruth was at home awaiting the outcome of the meeting between the other kinsman and Boaz. She had no idea the transaction had been done and that Boaz had just announced his engagement to her without her knowledge!

Ruth was about to become the bride of one of the most famous, wealthy and honourable men in Bethlehem and she didn't even know it!

Boaz had redeemed these two widows from their state of destitution and all that belonged to him would now also belong to Ruth because God had kept His promises through His servant Boaz. Their days of hunger and poverty would be no more.

What a day in the lives of these two widows! All the tears, sadness and sorrow would soon be replaced with inexpressible joy when the groom would come for his bride.

This is a beautiful picture of the grace of God found in Jesus, His only Son and willing Servant,

> *"Fear not, for I have **redeemed** you;*
> *I have summoned you by name;*
> *you are **mine**."*
> *(Isaiah 43:1)*

Jesus paid for our redemption with his own precious blood.

The transaction was done at Calvary.

We belong to him.

As his blood bought people we are called the Bride of Christ.

We await that glorious day when He will come to receive us to His home in heaven.

There we will take our place as we share in the Marriage supper of the Lamb.

What a day in the life of the believer that will be!

You saw my need and You came..... Immanuel
You became like me, so that I could become like You....
Jesus
You paid the price to set me free.....Redeemer
You are coming again....King
You are taking me to Your home....Father

'Blessed are those who are invited to the wedding supper of the Lamb.'
Rev.19:9

"Sing, O barren woman,
you who never bore a child
burst into song, shout for joy,
you who were never in labour;
because more are the children of the
desolate woman than of her who has a husband," Says the LORD,

"Enlarge the place of your tent,
stretch your tent curtains wide,
do not hold back;
lengthen your cords,
strengthen your stakes.
For you will spread out to the right and
to the left;
your descendants will dispossess
nations
and settle in their desolate cities..."
        Isaiah 54:1-3

Ruth 4:13
*Then he went to her, and the L*ORD *enabled her to conceive, and she gave birth to a son.*

When we look at the story of Ruth in Scripture we are given no details as to how long she had been married to Mahlon or how long she had been widowed. What we do know is, she had no children and her sister-in-law Orpah remained childless also.

In the Sovereignty and providence of God neither of these Moabite women had children to their Hebrew husbands. Had Orpah given birth to a son the story of Ruth would be null and void.

It is with wonderment and awe we read of Ruth having a child and a son at that!

How she must have longed for a child when she was married to Mahlon. The disappoinment when yet another month went by and Ruth wasn't pregnant must have been heart-breaking for them both.

She and barren Orpah probably shared their tears and frustration and looked to Naomi for comfort.

BUT ....*the* L*ORD*

Naomi and Ruth had returned to Bethlehem on hearing those same words and at that time it was because the L*ORD* had provided food in Israel. Now we read, *the L*ORD *enabled Ruth to conceive!*

How amazing is that?

Ruth realized now that God must have had a reason for her not conceiving in the past.
His purposes were beyond human understanding.
After all the questions, the pain of childlessness had been removed.
In God's will and in God's time, Ruth became a mother.
  Sometimes when we read of the barren women in Scripture such as Hannah and Elizabeth, we don't stop long enough and take note of the wonderful God we have. The One who alone holds the power to open barren wombs and allow for conception. His name is,

ELOHIM -
Creator,
Father, Son, Holy Spirit.

Heavenly Father,
You alone created the heavens and the earth and all that is in them.
You alone created mankind.
You give and You take away.
You open the eyes of the blind, the ears of the deaf, the mouths of the dumb.
The womb of the barren woman.
Blessed be the name of

The LORD

Sons are a heritage from the LORD**, children a reward from him. Ps. 127:3**

204

You turned my wailing into dancing; you removed my sackcloth and clothed me with
joy, that my heart may sing to you and not
be silent.

O LORD my God, I will give you thanks for
ever.

Ps. 30:11,12

Ruth 4:15
'For your daughter-in-law, who loves you and who is better than seven sons, has given him birth.

Ruth's story has taken us through grief, sorrow and tears. She has shown how women can make a difference.

Not only in their own families but in the wider community.

The Moabitess had walked into Bethlehem and an unknown future. Her faith and trust in God had given her a renewed sense of purpose and a reason to go on. The hope she had in her heart grew from a spark, into a flame of passion which desired to see YAHWEH in action.

She was the wind beneath Naomi's wings which gave Naomi also, a sense of better times ahead.

Ruth changed people's lives through her simplicity of faith. Just taking God at His word and applying it to daily living. Should Ruth's prayer be, "Give us this day our daily bread" that's what she expected. Literally!

Her marriage to Boaz had brought her into a royal family.
Her name would be listed in the lineage of Jesus.

David, her great-grandson, who wrote many of the Psalms quoted in this book, reflected perhaps not only on his own circumstances but also on the stories he had heard from his great-grandmother Ruth.

Here was a woman we would not have reckoned to one day meet in 'Our Father's House' but the Book of Ruth teaches us that the Grace of God reaches further than we expect or even think.

God's beckoning voice calls ordinary people living ordinary lives and bids them, 'Come.'

Ruth answered that call and great was her reward as she became,

a daughter of Abraham through faith
a redeemed child of God
and as such,
given
a new wardrobe - clothed in His Righteousness
a new name - no longer the Moabitess
a new family - the Royal family of Jesus
a new home - the great House of God
a new identity - child of the Father in heaven.

Redeemed.
Restored.
Renewed.

This is what God does for those
who are in Christ Jesus.

Heavenly Father, Your Grace knows no barriers.
Regardless of who we are, where we are or what we
are,
You can reach into the recesses of our very beings and
stir up a hunger for You.
You take us as we are and make us into the people
You want us to be.
With Your help may we continue in Your Word of
Truth and hunger and thirst after You.
May Your Holy Spirit fan the flame within our hearts
so that we will burn with desire for You.

Jesus said, "....Rejoice and be glad, be-
cause great is your reward in heaven...."
Matt.5:12

"....Rejoice that your names are written in
heaven."
Luke10:20

LORD you have assigned me my portion
and my cup; you have made my lot secure.
The boundary lines have fallen for me in
pleasant places; surely I have a delightful
inheritance.

     Ps. 16:5,6

Ruth 4:17
And they named him Obed.

The women, possibly neighbours and friends, had all gathered to visit the new-born and rejoice with Ruth and Naomi. Their focus seemed to be on Naomi which once again helps us to see that this story had much to do with the redemption of Elimelech's property and the continuation of his name.

Naomi who had left Moab bereft of her husband and sons had been given a son by her daughter -in-law

'who loved her and was better than seven sons'

As they looked at the wonderful gift which had been given to Naomi they raised their voices in praise and prayer and in naming the baby Obed, they said of him,

"May he become famous throughout Israel, He will renew your life and sustain you in your old age"

Blessing came from their lips for Naomi. How delighted they were she would now have a man about the house as she would grow older. Someone to provide and care for her.

Ruth had married an 'older' man but here was one who would be there for all of them at a later stage.

Obed was another 'man of Bethlehem' whose name meant 'Servant'. He would express in his life the same love and devotion to Naomi as Ruth his mother had done.

As the rightful heir to all Elimelech's property, the responsibility to safeguard his inheritance would eventually fall upon his shoulders.

His mother, father and grandmother had each made enormous sacrifices to keep the name of his grandfather in the history books and Obed would soon hear the story and do what would be expected of him.

This child would grow to be the blessing the people had prayed on the day of his birth,

He would indeed be famous in Bethlehem,
as the father of Jesse and the
grandfather of David, Israel's greatest King,
from whose line would come
the
Lord Jesus Christ.

Obed took his place in the gallery of the 'Men of Bethlehem' all of which were in the lineage of the Lord Jesus Christ,
The Bread of Life
the
Man of Bethlehem

Heavenly Father, all of these characters stepped up and took their place on the Your stage.
Each playing their role through the lines of Your written word.
Receiving the blessing of the promises because of their obedience.
Blessing others by kindness shown in very practical ways.

His master replied 'Well done, good and faithful servant!
        Matt. 25:21

The end of a matter is better than
it's beginning.
        Ecclesiastes 7:8

Ruth 4:14,16,17
The women said to Naomi:
"Praise be to the LORD, who this day has not left you without a kinsman-redeemer."
Then Naomi took the child, laid him in her lap and cared for him.
The women living there said, "Naomi has a son."

Naomi, when we first met her was a famine refugee. Her griefs and struggles led her to believe that God had forgotten her, two house moves three deaths in her family and parting with Orpah had taken its toll on this daughter of Abraham.

Her heart was so broken she had felt the need to call herself Mara. This name seemed more suitable for the bitter circumstances she had experienced during the previous years of her life.

When Naomi had come back to her home town of Bethlehem it was with empty hands and an empty heart, to an empty house. Alongside her was Ruth her daughter-in-law and at that time, Naomi did not realize the blessing she had in this young Moabite woman.

The future had looked dismal and uncertain and as the days and weeks rolled by she had returned to her former thoughts surrounding Ruth and what the future would hold for her, if anything.

Now, less than a year later,
she was holding a precious baby boy in her arms!

Because of the determination and strength of character displayed by Ruth in seeking to apply the law of the kinsman- redeemer to their situation, Naomi now 'had a son'.

All the doubts, fears and uncertainties she may have had, were swallowed up in praise and thanksgiving to YAHWEH, whose faithfulness and steadfast love shone through the features of this little gift which was laid upon her lap.

Naomi's faith in God during her trials of the past, had been enough to convince Ruth of the reality of the God of Israel and, because of Ruth's faith to believe God for the impossible, Naomi had now become a grandmother. She cared for the little boy, looking after his daily needs and probably singing songs she had once sung to her own children. This child was a gift from God. He was God's answer in keeping Elimelech's name alive in history and she would nurture him also in all those things concerning their wonderful covenant God, YAHWEH.

The young Moabitess had indeed brought blessing into Naomi's life such as she had never thought possible and there was singing once again in,

Ruth and Naomi's
HOUSE OF BREAD

Gracious Father we have witnessed You,
turning sorrow into joy,
despair into hope,
disappointment into delight.
The impossible becoming reality
and love beyond limits.
Thank-you!

*Because of your great love we are not con-
sumed, for your compassions never fail.
They are new every morning; great is your
faithfulness.*
    Lamentations 3:22,23

Blessed are the poor in spirit,
for theirs is the kingdom of heaven.
Blessed are those who mourn,
for they will be comforted.
Blessed are the meek,
for they will inherit the earth.
Blessed are those who hunger and thirst for righteousness,
for they will be filled.
Blessed are the merciful,
for they will be shown mercy.
Blessed are the pure in heart,
for they will see God.
Blessed are the peacemakers,
for they will be called the sons of God.
Blessed are those who are perse-
cuted because of righteousness,
for theirs is the kingdom of heaven.

Matthew 5:3-10

I trust you enjoyed the visit to

RUTH AND NAOMI'S

House

of

Bread

Marion